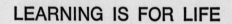

LEARNING IS FOR LIFE

Broadman Press / Nashville, Tennessee

RAYMOND M. RIGDON

Learning is for LIFE

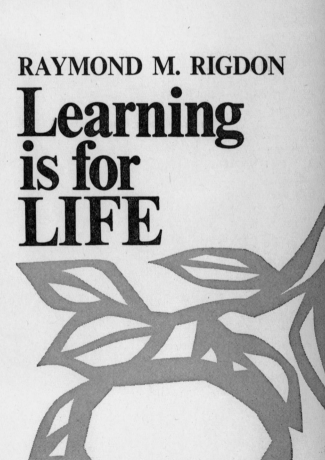

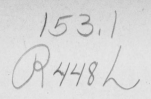

Library of Congress Catalog Card Number: 75–145985
Dewey Decimal Classification: 153.1
Printed in the United States of America
17.5Jy71KSP

Preface

This book grows out of a deep conviction that adults today must learn or perish. Of course, the alternative to learning is not to perish in a physical sense. Life will continue even for the adult who makes no effort to learn. But any adult in today's world who loses interest in learning faces perpetual frustration, personal failure, and oblivion.

Two false concepts discourage many adults from taking maximum advantage of their learning opportunities. The first is an assumption that one must return to school to learn. Although thousands of adults are currently enrolled in formal courses, meaningful learning is not restricted to the formal classroom.

A second false assumption is that learning is limited to the acquisition of facts. The increase in knowledge is one important type of learning, but there are other kinds which are equally essential to the well-rounded life in today's society.

The thesis of this book is that learning is imperative for

today's adult. A recurring theme of the book is that the average adult has far more learning opportunities each day than he realizes. By becoming alert to these learning opportunities and taking advantage of each as it comes, any adult can make life his classroom and the normal opportunities and frustrations of life the subject matter.

Why is learning an imperative for the modern adult. Until the reader finds truthful answers to this question, he may not fully understand the urgency to continue to learn. Thus the first chapter deals with the necessity to continue to learn throughout life.

Psychological, or emotional, factors which contribute to optimum learning are explored in Chapter 2.

Chapter 3 explores the real meaning of learning and kinds of learning which contribute to mature adulthood.

Several specific learning skills and how they can be developed are described in Chapters 4 through 9.

The final chapter explores changes predicted during the next few decades and the implications of those changes for adults and their need to learn.

The author invites the reader to join him in a thrilling exploration of the learning potential of adulthood.

Contents

CHAPTER 1
Learning Is for Living

Our grandparents assumed that preparation for life was achieved entirely during childhood and youth. When one became an adult, they believed, he ceased learning and began to live.

Big John Champion lived in Mecklenburg County, Virginia, fifty years ago. No one would have dared to suggest that Big John needed to continue to learn anything. Wealthy and highly respected by all who knew him, he ruled with a firm hand his family and the dozens of Negroes who worked his huge plantation.

And, as a matter of fact, he had few practical reasons for continuing to learn. His grade-school education, supplemented by years of practical experience, equipped him to transact business in his rural community. Government regulations, tax forms, and investment opportunities were relatively simple in his day.

Farming practices he learned from his father continued to be the accepted practices of his own day. Agricultural technology did not advance as much during Big John's entire lifetime as it has during each of the past dozen years.

The Richmond *Times Dispatch,* which reached his plantation home two days late, was his only regular contact with the world outside Mecklenburg County. That world outside Mecklenburg County exerted little influence upon the daily activities of Big John and his friends.

Big John's world changed little during his entire lifetime. He mastered that world during his first thirty years. After thirty, he felt no need to struggle with new ideas or strange concepts. Adulthood was for living and not for learning.

Our World Today

Many dramatic changes have taken place in American society since Big John's time. Radio and television transmit news to and from the far places of the world almost the moment it happens. Massive jets transport passengers across the continent in only a fraction of the time that it took Big John to travel by buggy the eighty miles to Richmond. Sensational developments in agricultural technology long since have made obsolete almost every farming technique known in Big John's day.

Man-made satellites orbit the earth to bounce television programs from one continent to another. The radar antenna for Tel-Star I, the first communications satellite, was so powerful that it defied imagination. If placed in New York and beamed in the right direction, scientists say, Tel-Star's antenna could detect a gnat batting its wings in Bombay, India. Today we have communication satellites even more powerful than Tel-Star I.

Accompanying these changes has been a drastic change in the attitude of adults toward learning. No longer do intelligent persons assume that preparation for life is achieved entirely during childhood and youth. Neither do they believe that when one becomes an adult, he ceases learning and begins to live. The world is changing so rapidly that adults are forced to continue to learn to keep up, as best they can, with all that is going on around them.

Millions of American adults are continuing their learning by going back to school. Margie Savoy, in an Associated Press news feature said:

All over America grown-ups are lugging school books—18 million of them, teenagers to granddads, are enrolled this year in colleges, on-the-job classes, trade schools, seminars, union schools, army schools, industry workshops.

This doesn't count 9 million poring over correspondence courses, thousands concentrating on educational TV classes, millions taking lessons from tutors or attending lecture series in community centers, churches, and clubs.

More people were in formal adult classes last year than passed through the gates of all major league baseball clubs. One out of three who voted in the last election was going to school.

'Going back to school' has become the national pastime.

They're studying everything from the basic three R's to Russian 18th Century literature—in Russia. Some courses are aimed at bringing illiterates to the level where they can take jobs or go into semi-skilled training. Others are sharpening Ph.D.'s for atomic research.[1]

Why Are Adults Continuing to Learn?

What has caused this dramatic change in the attitude of American adults toward learning? Educators and sociologists give many reasons. Four are especially pertinent.

1. Struggle for Survival

Of all the reasons which can be given for the increased interest of adults in learning, none is more significant than this. Self-preservation is one of man's basic instincts. Primitive man fought wild animals and battled warring tribes to maintain his existence. Our pioneer forefathers braved dangers and toiled ceaselessly to carve out of the wild forests farms which would sustain themselves and their loved ones.

Today's American adult is not called upon to brave the physical dangers encountered by primitive man or even by our pioneer forefathers. Man has made giant strides toward conquering the physical universe. Giant forests have been transformed into massive shopping centers. Wild animals are kept in zoos. Indian raids are limited to refrigerators in the Indians' own homes.

Yet man's struggle for survival continues. Technological and scientific developments are frontiers which must be conquered by millions of today's professional and working people. Dr. Jones must study constantly to keep abreast with medical progress if he is to have a steady stream of patients crowding his waiting room. If Bill Hollingsworth succeeds with his hole-in-the-wall TV repair shop, he must study the latest magazines and books on television. Roy Crane, who has not missed a day from his factory job in twenty years, was notified that changes soon to be made in his plant will make his job obsolete. His option was to learn a completely new job and stay with his company or to look elsewhere for employment.

The struggle for survival continues to be one of man's most potent drives. The weapons he uses today are textbooks, trade journals, company-sponsored seminars, educational TV courses, and the experiences of life itself.

2. Concern to Understand and Adjust to Changes

Rapid changes in many other areas of life provide additional stimuli to learning.

The dropping of the first atomic bomb forced all thoughtful adults into numerous significant learning experiences. Feelings of awe over the fantastic power the bomb unleashed motivated millions to read avidly newspaper and magazine articles dealing with the power and potential of the split atom. Concern over what seemed to be the ultimate in man's inhuman treatment of man stimulates scores of thoughtful discussions on the moral implications of the atomic bomb. Fear of fallout drove millions of American homeowners to learn all they could about family-sized fallout shelters.

More recently, explorations into space have stimulated a fantastic amount of learning on the part of adults. Most of us have seen with our own eyes, thanks to television, men walking on the moon. We have heard these men talking, and the sounds of their voices reached us almost as quickly as did the astonished comments of family members viewing television with us. Newspapers, magazines, and other news media have bombarded us with simplified explanations of many of the mysteries of the universe. As a result, most of us can discuss with some degree of intelligence the characteristics of weightlessness, the dangers of reentry into space, and other phenomena which, until a short time ago, baffled even the most learned scientists.

As our universe has grown larger, our world has grown smaller. Quick communication and rapid transportation have made the world one neighborhood. The ten o'clock evening news brings reports from the far places of the world. Documentary TV programs help us see the news and newsmakers of the world and to hear informative interpretations of events.

Home conveniences thrust other learnings upon us. Shopping for a new stereo has provided many adults interesting learning opportunities in the characteristics of sound. Televised weather reports open up for us the whole field of meteorology. Even struggling to start a power lawn mower has provoked scores of harassed suburbanites to learn something of the baffling yet intriguing mysteries of the gasoline engine.

One cannot live in a dynamic and rapidly changing

society like ours without learning many new things each day. But he can determine how alert he will be to the scores of learning opportunities which bombard him and how much effort he will exert to gain the most from those opportunities.

3. Desire to Use Profitably Increased Leisuretime

Increased leisuretime is another tremendous stimulant to learning. Most of us feel that we have little time which can properly be called leisure. Our days and evenings are crowded to the limit with the responsibilities of our jobs, homes, churches, and communities.

Yet, leisure rapidly is becoming the American way of life. As a nation, we have more free time than was available to any other generation of adults in modern history.

Many factors are responsible for this increased leisure. Progress in technology and working conditions have reduced the number of hours we are spending on our jobs. The average employee today works thirty fewer hours a week than did his grandfather.

Reduced retirement ages and enforced retirement policies are responsible for the increased leisure of additional hundreds of thousands of persons each year. Dr. Gaines S. Dobbins, prominent Southern Baptist Christian educator, has said that a man today needs to think of his career in three stages. These stages are (1) getting ready for one's career, (2) pursuing one's career, and (3) finding profitable ways to spend one's time after retirement.

An increase in the average life span also is increasing

the amount of leisuretime available to American senior citizens. Since 1900, the average length of life has increased almost twenty years. It is important to note, however, that people, generally speaking, are not living much longer today than they did a century ago. The average person who lives to be sixty today will average about seventeen more years—about two years more than in 1900. People are not living much longer today than they did formerly; but more of them are living out the normal life span. Due to the reduction of mortality in infancy and the conquest of such diseases as diphtheria, many more persons now than formerly are living out their full four score and ten years.[2]

This increased leisure is challenging many more adults to continue learning. Many retirees, active throughout their vocational lives, are finding time now to do the reading and studying they previously felt that they did not have the time to do.

4. Desire for Personal Improvement

For many centuries, thoughtful persons attributed to the gods and the spirits, both good and bad, those urges which drive people to action. In more recent years, psychologists have labeled those urges as motivations.

Our motivations, psychologists say, are inner drives to achieve goals which we consider to be worthy. Many times those goals are not perceived on a conscious level. Our motivations may be confused or even contradictory. Nevertheless, these unconscious, confused, and often contradictory motivations are drives to struggle toward many things beyond our reach.

One motivation common to all of us is the motivation for self-fulfilment. We feel the urge to reach out for goals beyond ourselves, goals which call for personal growth.

Malcolm S. Knowles [3] has said:

There is convincing evidence that this urge (for continuing personal growth) continues to operate throughout normal life. The mature adult who 'can see no future' for himself is a familiar and pitiful figure in psychological clinics. Without some future to grow to, life becomes less than worthwhile. Even in old age there is apparently a need to keep growing. Recent studies of retired persons reveal that those who have some secondary purpose in life toward which they can continue to strive succeed in making a happy adjustment. Those who have not mapped out new directions to explore suffer intensely and may even die.

Of all the reasons which challenge adults to continue to learn, one of the most basic and enduring is this urge for continuing personal growth. Not all adults have the same goals for personal growth. It is understandable, therefore, that adults would express in a variety of ways this search for self-fulfilment. Many adults aspire to continue to grow intellectually; this urge drives them to read widely and to converse on scholarly subjects. Other adults may aspire to be an expert fisherman, the best whittler at the country store, or the best tomato grower in town.

Our goals vary widely, but all of us are reaching out for personal goals which represent our desire for self-fulfilment. These goals, like magnets, draw us into many different types of learning situations.

Let's Look Ahead

Most of us associate learning with school, textbooks, and teachers. This is understandable, since learning traditionally has been considered almost exclusively an academic pursuit.

In the pages ahead, we shall explore another kind of learning. It is a type of learning which is available to every normal adult regardless of how much or how little schooling he has had. It is available to adults in school and adults out of school forever. It is available to busy businessmen and harassed housewives, to active career women, and to well-dressed professional men. Both white-collar workers and blue-collar workers will find help in this book.

The theme of this book is that learning must continue throughout life. The alternative is personal frustration and deterioration. In a real sense, one must continue to learn or perish as a person of integrity and wholeness. Subsequent chapters deal with ways adults can use daily informal learning opportunities in learning to live more creative and successful lives.

This is not a book for casual, informal reading. Unless the reader seriously desires to learn throughout life, he would do well to close the book now and look at the comic page of today's newspaper.

On the other hand, if the reader has a serious interest

in continuing to grow, the pages ahead offer a compelling invitation to learning.

PERSONAL LEARNING ACTIVITIES

1. How alert are you to informal learning opportunities? Think through your experiences of the past few days and identify three or four special learning opportunities which you have had. Did you take full advantage of each? What can you do to continue your learnings in these areas?

2. Identify two or three crucial issues in the news. Go to the public library and read all you can find on each of these issues. Define your personal feelings about each of the issues.

3. Visit a session of your city council and observe its operation. Talk with your councilman about the work of the council.

4. Secure from the public library one or more books explaining the electrical and the plumbing systems of your house. Study these until you feel competent to make simple repairs in these systems.

GROUP DISCUSSION STARTERS

1. Why is learning more important for adults today than it was for their grandparents fifty years ago?

2. What formal learning opportunities are available to adults in your community? (Have someone investigate each and report on courses offered, schedule of classes, tuition, etc.)

3. What informal learning opportunities are available?

(Lead the group in a discussion of educational television programs they have seen lately. Have someone check the TV schedules for the coming week to identify forthcoming programs which will provide special opportunities for learning.)

4. What are some of the main obstacles which prevent you from learning more than you do?

5. What can you do to overcome these obstacles?

6. What will you do?

NOTES

1. Margie Savoy, "Americans Are Going Back to School," AP Newsfeature, *The Nashville Tennessean*, January 16, 1965.

2. Pressey and Huhlen, *Psychological Development Through the Life Span* (New York: Harper & Brothers, 1939) p. 4.

3. Malcolm S. Knowles, *Informal Adult Education* (New York: Association Press, 1950), p. 13.

CHAPTER 2
Freedom to Learn

We find in Hebrews 12:1, a graphic picture of an athlete running a race. The coach urges the runner to rid himself of encumberances which would reduce his speed.

In beginning our quest for meaningful learning throughout life, we need first to consider a general life pattern which facilitates optimum learning. As is true in the Christian life, so in learning there are encumberances which reduce our speed and limit our distance. Frustrations, tensions, and anxieties, for example, not only make concentration difficult, but they actually deplete us of the physical and emotional energies essential to successful learning.

The best way to avoid these encumberances which impair learning is to strive to develop certain personal qualities which make learning easier. Generally speaking, most of these qualities can be grouped under two headings. They are *growth toward maturity* and *the achievement of developmental tasks*. Although admittedly there is some overlapping in these two areas, each has a sufficiently clear focus to justify individual consideration.

In each we find clusters of traits which, in themselves, can be worthy learning goals. If you are serious in your intentions to continue meaningful learning throughout life, your first major learning exercise is to identify, as you read the remainder of this chapter, a minimum of six traits which you need to concentrate on developing. As you identify each, pause and think through your personal strengths and weaknesses in that particular area. Make notes on ideas which come to you as to ways you can develop or strengthen the traits which you have identified. At the end of the chapter, you will find suggestions on how the development of these traits can become worthy learning goals for the weeks immediately ahead.

Growth Toward Maturity

Several false concepts of maturity frequently conceal its true meanings. Perhaps the chief misconception is that complete maturity can be achieved. Contrary to popular opinion, no sane person is completely mature or completely immature. When we say that a person is mature, actually what we mean is that, with some degree of consistency, he reacts in mature ways to myriad problems, opportunities, and tensions in life. An immature person reacts immaturely to life's ceaseless demands.

Another false concept of maturity is that it is synonymous with adulthood. The word "adult" comes from the Latin word meaning grown up. The assumption is that when one reaches this age, he is capable of coping successfully with life's persistent irritations and inevitable frustrations. On the contrary, the alarming increase in mental and moral breakdowns among adults attests their need for continuing growth toward maturity.

Another false concept equates maturity with superior intelligence. Certainly the world would be a better place if all persons with superior intelligence were sufficiently mature to use their intelligence constructively. While many persons with superior intelligence are inspiring examples of maturity, the Adolph Hitlers and the Karl Marxes of our time challenge the assumption that intelligence and maturity are the same thing.

Many persons accept religious zeal as a valid criterion of maturity. It is true that a genuine Christian experience and an ever deepening faith do provide the most substantial foundation for growth toward maturity, but some people who seem to display fruits of the Christian faith lack the roots. Thus religious zeal *per se* is not the same as maturity.

If these popular concepts are false, what, then, is the real meaning of maturity? Although it is difficult in a brief space to give a full description, let us consider five characteristics of a mature person.

1. *A mature person is guided by worthy, long-range goals rather than immediate desires.* All voluntary conduct is an effort to achieve goals of some kind. The nature

and enduring quality of those goals reflects the degree of one's maturity.

Al and Joe work together on a construction project. Al has a happy disposition and takes life as it comes. Most of his goals are expressed in spur-of-the moment decisions to do such things as buy a boat, make a weekend trip to the beach, or spend lavishly on a gift for a friend. He has no long-range goals which help determine daily choices and decisions.

Joe is a devoted family man. One of his chief goals in life is to provide for his family a comfortable home in the suburbs. As the outright purchase of a home seems out of the question, Joe has bought a lot and is attempting to build the house himself. Almost every decision he makes involving the use of free time or money is influenced by his long-range goal to complete the house for his family. One indication of his maturity is his consistency in making immediate decisions in the light of this long-range objective.

However, one may consistently make immediate decisions in the light of long-range objectives and still be an immature person. The quality of those goals is a determining factor. The owner of a corner grocery store may harbor deep hatred for a competitor and resolve to "get even" each time an opportunity presents itself. This determination becomes a long-range goal which influences his daily conduct. Yet one would not consider this long-range goal to be an indication of maturity, for the long-range goals of a mature person are unselfishly related to the interests and welfare of others.

2. *A mature person is able without frustration to accept the authority of others and the limitations of circumstances.* Freedom, a cherished American tradition, sometimes is misinterpreted as license to act in an unrestrained manner. The essence of freedom is the opportunity to choose one's way of life. By no means does it remove the necessity for discipline or restrictions in the free exercise of that way of life. One of the ironies of life is that the more we exercise our freedom in choosing ambitious objectives, the more we subject ourselves to the disciplines and restrictions essential to achieving those objectives.

In varying degrees and circumstances, all of us are subject to the authority of others and to the limitations of circumstances. The mature person is one who is able without frustration to accept that authority and those circumstances. Although he may strive vigorously to change conditions, his philosophy of life helps him accept those conditions as long as they are necessary.

3. *A mature person is able to see and to accept persons as they are. He does not judge them by standards of what he thinks they ought to be.* All of us live among imperfect people. Honesty compels us to admit, moreover, that our own imperfections are greater than those of many persons with whom we associate. Almost everyone is tempted at some time to become irritated by the imperfections and shortcomings of a friend, a colleague at work, or even a

family member. One mark of maturity is the capacity to see these imperfections in the light of the dignity and supreme worth of the person displaying them. This does not mean that the mature person may not have concern for helping someone else overcome certain imperfections. It means that he doesn't permit another's limitations to blind him to that person's good qualities and infinite worth in the sight of God.

4. *A mature person is able to love others so satisfyingly that he is less dependent upon being loved.* The desire to be loved and accepted is basic in human experience. Psychologists tell us that this desire is so strong that failure to be loved and accepted leads to many types of personality maladjustments.

A mark of maturity is the cultivation of interests and love outside oneself. These interests and loves may take a variety of forms, such as love for family, church loyalty, interest in Boy Scouts, or devotion to the cause of world missions. As a person cultivates such loves and interests, he becomes less dependent upon praise, personal recognition, and the frequent expressions of love and appreciation from persons around him.

5. *A mature person is able to adjust to, and even grow as a result of, life's inevitable frustrations.* Hardships, disappointments, and the death of loved ones are, at some time in life, as inevitable as the rising sun. Frequently, one's reaction to these experiences is far more important to his future well-being than are the experiences.

Tragedy struck suddenly in the heart of Midville. A

drunken driver lost control of his car and crashed into a cluster of students, killing two teen-age girls. Ann's parents were distraught with grief and embittered toward God for permitting their daughter to be taken in this way. Mary's parents, equally grieved, resolved, with God's help to promote alcohol education among high school students, with the hope eventually of saving other parents from the grief which they were experiencing. The conduct of Mary's parents reflects true maturity.

Achieving Developmental Tasks

While growth toward maturity is a lifelong process, the need for growth in certain areas is characteristic of specific periods of adulthood. These special needs are known as developmental tasks. R. J. Havighurst, leading exponent of developmental psychology, describes a developmental task as a need which usually arises at a certain period in the life of an individual which, if met, usually leads to happiness and success with a later task, and, if not met, usually leads to unhappiness, maladjustment, and difficulty at a later task.

Let us consider some of the developmental tasks of three periods of adulthood.

1. Young Adulthood

Of all periods of life, early adulthood is the fullest of teachable moments and the emptiest of efforts to teach. It is a time of special sensitivity and unusual readiness of the person to learn. Early adulthood, the period from eighteen to thirty, usually contains marriage, the first pregnancy, the first serious full-time job, the first illnesses of children, the first experience of furnishing or buying or building a house and the first venturing of the child off to school. If ever people are motivated to learn and to learn quickly, it is at times such as these.[1]

This description of characteristic experiences of young adults suggests several developmental tasks. Let us consider some of them.

Adjustment to living with a spouse is one of the big developmental tasks of this period. Of all of the adjustments of life, perhaps the greatest, except for the conversion experience itself, is the fusing of one's life with that of another and learning to live harmoniously with that person.

Betty and Bob were blissfully happy the day of their wedding. Little did they realize the adjustments which must be made before their marriage would be anchored in a solid foundation. Bob was thrifty; Betty liked to spend freely. Bob was accustomed to leaving dirty clothes where he took them off; Betty wanted them placed immediately in the dirty clothes hamper. Bob's idea of a good time was to don old clothes and go fishing; Betty enjoyed dining out frequently or inviting friends in for a lavish meal.

Adjustments to differences such as these are the foundations on which lasting marriages are made. Sometimes these adjustments are not compromises by either or both mates. Adjustments may come as one partner comes to realize that the lovable qualities of his or her mate far outweigh those irritating habits.

Learning the role of a parent is another developmental

task of young adults. While Bob and Betty were learning to adjust to each other, they learned that Betty was pregnant. When the baby came, they found themselves confronted with additional adjustments. Social and recreational activities had to be curtailed. The salary check, already stretched to the limit, had to provide for a third person. Bob became secretly jealous of the baby for claiming so much of Betty's time and interest.

While Bob and Betty were struggling with their developmental tasks, Sue, Betty's sister, was struggling with a developmental task of her own. A shattered romance seemed to have wrecked permanently her dreams of marriage and a family. She was having to learn to support herself and to live alone. Although of an entirely different character, her developmental task was as difficult for her as were Betty's and Bob's for them.

Vocational achievement is an important developmental task for the young adult breadwinner. Many young husbands realize that the progress one makes vocationally before he reaches the age of forty usually determines the approximate level to which he will climb later in life. This creates heavy pressure upon many men to work long hours and to make heavy sacrifices "to become established." Sometimes this pressure leads to conflict with family responsibilities, and the resulting tensions between husband and wife make more difficult the achieving of their developmental task of marital adjustment.

Young adulthood also is a period of moral testing. Although not a developmental task exclusively for this age group, the young adult does undergo severe moral testing. It is profoundly true that the way he or she reacts to this testing determines significantly his or her effectiveness in dealing with similar situations later in life.

2. The Middle Years

In *The Creative Years*, Reuel L. Howe [2] offers penetrating insight into the psychology of the middle period of adulthood. In the opening chapter, he tells the story of Dick Foster, "an uneasy husband, confused father, moderately successful businessman." While returning home on a commuter train after a hectic day in the office, Dick muses over his failures and frustrations at home, in the office, and in life generally. In succeeding chapters, the author uses the specific problems of Dick Foster to interpret problems common, to some degree, to the experiences of most middle-aged adults. Through the discussion of these problems, he describes ways in which this middle period can be the most creative years of life.

One of the principal developmental tasks of this middle period of life is the reconciling of ideals to reality. Youth and young adulthood may be characterized as periods of dreaming. Ambitions frequently run high. Although young adulthood may be a period of hard knocks, failures do not always suppress the hope of a brighter day tomorrow.

Frequently, during middle age comes the realization that many of one's vocational dreams and ambitions perhaps will never be realized. Some adults who once dreamed of setting the world afire are forced to admit, at least to themselves, that school friends have gone far beyond them vocationally. Reluctantly, many of these middle-aged adults realize that perhaps they will never emerge from their present routine existence.

Middle age may also be a period of adjusting to reality earlier aspirations of "a perfect home and model children." Although one's home life may be happy and his children typical teen-agers, Johnny's aversion to schoolwork and Sue's affair with the Lester boy are inconsistent with their parents' earlier dreams of a son who would be a straight A student and a beautiful daughter who would never be a problem to them.

Adjustment to one's major responsibility in life is another developmental task of the middle years. Regardless of how high one climbs on the ladder of success, usually it is during this middle adult period that he carries his heaviest load vocationally. Learning to carry that load with a minimum of tension and maximum efficiency is a developmental task which can influence every other area of life.

These middle years usually bring the heaviest financial strain of life. Life for many fathers beyond forty becomes a constant struggle to stretch the salary check until the next payday. One harassed father commented facetiously that he finally had concluded that his family simply could not afford to have a last week in every month.

Preparation for retirement is another important developmental task of this period. Medical, educational, and religious leaders have come to realize the great importance of preparation if one is to make a satisfactory transition into the experience of retirement. Hobbies and other interests need to be developed or continued from earlier life. Friends need to be cultivated. Adequate financial preparation needs to be made for the time when the regular salary check will cease to come. In these and many other ways the middle-aged adult needs to be planning carefully for the reality of retirement.

3. After Retirement

Although it is difficult to place rigid age limits on any period of life, it is virtually impossible to affix an age at which time one passes from middle age into the final period of life. Individual differences are so great that some people begin to show signs of aging much earlier than do others of the same chronological age.

The time of retirement, because it introduces so many changes, is perhaps the best point to use in separating middle age from what increasingly is being thought of as the golden age of life. And even this golden age is not without its own developmental tasks.

One of the greatest developmental tasks of this golden period of life often is psychological adjustment to retirement itself. Persons who have lived busy lives and have been accustomed to major responsibilities frequently find it difficult to adjust to a diminished work load or to complete unemployment.

Finding new ways to fill one's time pleasantly and

profitably is another major developmental task of this period after retirement. Many retirees are successful in finding other responsibilities which challenge their creative initiative and their desire to be useful. Increasingly, churches and communities are offering persons in this group expanded opportunities to participate in worthwhile activities.

Adjustment to declining health and to the loss of a mate are perhaps the most crucial developmental tasks of most aging adults. Although progress in the field of geriatrics is responsible for the continuing good health of many older adults, with increasing age, one's organism shows decreasing ability to maintain normal conditions and greater resistance to recovery if these internal conditions have been disturbed. Thus, adjustment to failing health and the loss of a mate represent two of the most difficult developmental tasks of this or of any other period in life.

Conclusion

By no means are we saying that a person must be completely mature and fully adjusted to his developmental tasks before he can learn effectively. Learning is possible to almost all animate beings.

But to the adult who is seriously interested in continuing to learn, it is profoundly true that the person who is growing toward maturity and meeting his developmental tasks is more likely to continue to learn effectively throughout life.

PERSONAL LEARNING ACTIVITIES

1. Review the notes you made, in reading this chapter, on personal qualities which you need to develop or strengthen. For example, one goal might be: I will learn to be more patient in dealing with irritating or frustrating situations. Now reduce these goals to the ones on which you are willing to work seriously at this time.

2. Rewrite the goals you have selected, and place the list in a private place, such as your wallet.

3. During the next several weeks, look for opportunities to try to develop the traits you have selected as learning goals. Try experimental behavior patterns in trying to develop each.

4. At least once each week, review your goals and evaluate your performance in achieving each. Do not be discouraged by occasional failures. Remember, you may have to overcome some negative traits which have developed over a period of many years. Adults do not change their behavior patterns easily, but they can learn new behavior patterns at any age—if they are willing to try hard enough!

GROUP DISCUSSION STARTERS

1. What is the relationship between maturity and learning?

2. How does failure to achieve developmental tasks influence learning?

3. When crises come, why do some people "rise to the occasion" while others "just go up in the air?"

4. Evaluate each characteristic of maturity described in this chapter. Why is each a sign of maturity?

5. What special learnings are needed to achieve the developmental tasks of young adulthood? of middle adulthood? of older adulthood?

NOTES

1. R. J. Havighurst, *Human Development and Education* (New York: Longman, Green, and Co., 1952), p. 257.

2. Reuel L. Howe, *The Creative Years* (Greenwich: Seabury Press, 1959).

CHAPTER 3
How We Learn

Before we consider specific methods of learning, we need to look briefly at learning itself. What do we mean by learning? Are there different kinds of learning? What are some factors which influence learning? An understanding of problems like these can help us greatly in our efforts to sharpen our learning skills.

In exploring these problems, we are forced to admit that educational psychologists are not in complete agreement on what learning is. Bugelski [1] cautions:

We cannot turn to the learning psychologists for a set of mature, sweeping, internally consistent statements which will offer us the framework we need to consider our practical problems. . . . The point is that no systematic theory of learning exists now which accounts for all the phenomena that goes on in my classroom. There is not even a satisfactory definition of learning itself.

An Example of Learning

Inasmuch as we do not have a commonly accepted definition of learning, let us consider an actual learning experience. From an analysis of this incident, we may gain some understanding of what learning is.

A mother was harassed daily by what seemed to be the "incessant squabbling" between her six-year-old son and his eight-year-old sister. For months she sought to cope with the problem by dealing, usually with an angry outburst, with each situation as it arose. In a calmer moment one day she asked herself why her children had so many disagreements. For the first time she realized that there might be an underlying cause. She resolved to try to discover that cause and to correct the problem.

With this learning goal in mind, she began to observe more objectively the squabbles to discover, if possible, types of situations which usually caused them. After studying several outbursts, she discovered that they usually came when the older sister was doing something the younger brother was unable to achieve.

Through conversation with friends and reading material on child psychology, she discovered that younger brothers frequently feel keenly the competition with older sisters and that their subsequent feelings of inadequacy often lead to hostile behavior. A possible solution, one writer suggested, is to help the younger brother find ways in which he can excel.

She began to do this with her own son and, to her deep satisfaction, her problem of sibling squabbling was greatly reduced. She had learned a valuable lesson in child psychology.

The Anatomy of Learning

In this experience we find three elements which seem to be present in most learning experiences. Some psychologists say that they are present in every learning experience and that they are the essence of learning itself. They are (1) recognition of a need, (2) a conscious effort to meet that need and (3) a feeling of satisfaction over the result. Let's analyze these three factors.

1. Recognition of a Need

First, there was a recognition of a need. The mother realized there must be an underlying cause for the behavior problems in her home. She felt a need to discover that cause. Unfortunately, we do not always bring to a conscious level our frustrations, irritations, and exasperations. When they are brought to a conscious level and we resolve to do something about them, our frustrations, irritations, and exasperations frequently are beginning points for creative learning experiences.

Many times this first step, the recognition of a need, is manifested in a less dramatic way. It may be simply an awareness of a need for more information on a subject or a desire for the answer to a question. In formal study, this is the usual form in which a felt need expresses itself.

2. *Specific Action to Meet the Need*

Had the mother been satisfied simply to recognize the manifestation of her problem, she would not have had a significant learning experience. She resolved to find the real problem and to do something about it. Through observation, she discovered that her basic problem was her son's feeling of competition with his older sister. Through reading and conversation with friends she discovered that an effective way to handle the problem might be to help her son find ways in which he could excel. When the mother tried out the hypothesis, she found indeed that it worked.

In normal learning experiences, there must be some overt effort to meet a need. This overt effort may be expressed in study, in observation, in inquiry, in personal meditation, or in countless other ways. However expressed, the essence of learning is struggle to meet a felt need.

3. *Feeling of Satisfaction*

The final step in the mother's learning experience was a feeling of satisfaction over reducing tension in her family and helping her son meet one of his own needs.

This final step is important in any learning experience, for it helps us realize that we have acquired information, insight, or skill which can be used in similar situations in the future.

Kinds of Learning

The kinds of learning are so varied as to defy neat classifications. Three kinds are especially useful in informal adult education.

1. *The Acquisition of Knowledge*

Although the gaining of knowledge is not the only kind of learning, it is one of the most valuable. We live in a rapidly changing world. Unless we regularly add to our store of knowledge, we soon lose our ability to cope with the normal problems in a rapidly changing social order. The intelligent adult needs to keep abreast with developments in community, national, and world affairs. He needs at least a general knowledge of significant developments in science and technology.

An important personal skill is determining how well facts should be learned. There are levels of learning, and one does not need to learn some things as thoroughly as he needs to learn other things. The seven levels of learning [2] are:

Awareness—the knowledge that certain information is available from a specific source if and when needed.

Recognition—the ability to recognize certain facts and identify their source and normal relationships.

Recitation—the ability to reproduce the facts from memory.

Comprehension—a general understanding of the meanings communicated by the facts.

Use—the ability to use the facts intelligently.

Generalization—the ability to make certain valid generalizations based on the facts.

Internalization—an integration of the facts into personal thought patterns and behavior patterns.

2. Problem Solving

Problem solving is another kind of learning. Although knowledge and understanding are involved, basically this is a struggle to deal constructively with persistent problems in one's daily life and work.

During recent years, much attention has been given to steps in creative problem solving. Out of this study have come several general steps. They are: (1) identify and state the specific problem; (2) investigate the source of the problem and ways it manifests itself; (3) consider several possible ways for overcoming the problem and list the advantages and disadvantages of each; (4) select and follow through on what seems to be the best course of action; and (5) evaluate the results. These steps are discussed more fully in Chapter 6.

These general steps, if followed intelligently, can help solve many problems and make it possible to experience many thrilling learning experiences.

3. The Development of Skills

One of the most exciting types of learning is skill development. Basically, a skill is the ability to perform successfully in a particular area of life. Certainly this includes manual skills. Many adults have thrilling learning experiences as they seek to develop hobbies or skills in carpentry and other manual activities.

But we make a mistake if we limit skills to manual activities. Equally as important are other personal skills. These include such things as the ability to perform successfully in psychological adjustments and social relationships. There are skills in telling a joke, engaging in meaningful conversation, listening, dealing with conflict situations, and persuading someone to one's own viewpoint. Each of these and many other skills offer most adults learning opportunities unlimited.

Factors Which Influence Learning

Several factors influence learning. Three of the most important are motivation, concentration, and application.

1. Motivation

Almost all psychologists agree that little if any significant learning takes place unless one has a desire to learn. In approaching any learning situation, therefore, one might ask such questions as these: Why should I bother to learn this? What's in it for me? How will my life be better from having learned this?

Our motivations are so complicated that we can seldom, if ever, say that we have only one reason for wanting to do a thing. Usually we have multiple reasons, many of which we are not consciously aware. It is possible, however, to recognize some broad general desires which motivate most of us. With these in mind, we are better able to understand and utilize our motivations.

Self-realization is one of our basic desires which motivates learning. We each have some kind of a mental image, usually unclear and on an unconscious level, of the kind of person we want to be. This unclear mental image leads us to do many things. If we take time to clarify the image of the kind of a person we want to be, that image can be a wholesome drive for learnings necessary to become that kind of a person.

We also want to love and to be loved. This basic desire stimulates us to engage in many activities such as marrying, having a family, relating to friends. A conscious recognition of these desires helps us increase our efforts to achieve certain related learning experiences.

We have other basic drives, each spawning countless urges, desires, aspirations. All of these lead to learning experiences. Some express themselves in such desires as to be able to converse intelligently, to remove a conflict situation in interpersonal relations, to get a promotion, to better understand what's happening in the world. All of these desires motivate important learnings.

2. Concentration

Many experiments have proved conclusively that concentration plays an important part in learning. Moreover, just average concentration produces less than average learning. Intense concentration greatly increases the quantity of learning which takes place. Staton [3] explains it this way:

The relationship between learning and attention is not simply in direct ratio. Fifty percent attention does not result in fifty percent learning, etc. Rather, the curve of learning sags low for most of the mere attention period, but rises sharply at the extreme limit of attention, which is concentration. Where normal attention ceases and concentration begins, there the learning curve shoots steeply upward, and thereafter, the more intense the concentration the more rapid and effective the learning.

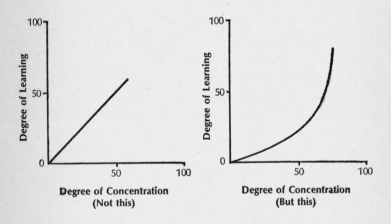

The above graph explains this phenomenon. It would seem that graph A would picture the learning curve. In this graph, 50 percent concentration seems to produce 50 percent learning. This is not the case, however. Figure B is the true learning curve. Note that most significant learning comes with a concentration of 75 to 100 percent, while little significant learning occurs with less than a 50 percent concentration.

This curve underscores the value of good conditions for learning. The radio or TV may not consciously disrupt our learning, yet we see what may happen if it cuts down our degree of concentration.

3. Application

In the final analysis, no learning is made permanent unless we put it into practice. This suggests the need to find ways in which we can use anything we learn.

The first step may be to review the material learned. The forgetting curve shoots up sharply soon after we have learned something. It is good, therefore, to review material several times at intervals of several days and weeks. Several studies have been made to determine scientifically the optimum plan for reviewing material to learn it permanently. Growing out of one of those studies is this suggestion: Learn the original material; review two days later, five days after that, ten days after that, and twenty days after that. Then throw your notes away because the material will be yours for life.[4]

In addition to reviewing the material, find opportunities as soon as possible and as often as possible to use what you have learned. Even to relate it to someone in conversation is helpful. The nature of the content learned helps to determine ways it can be used.

The important thing to remember is: *if you don't use it, you will lose it.*

PERSONAL LEARNING ACTIVITIES

1. Identify and review three meaningful learning experiences you have had during the past week. What kinds of learning were involved?

2. Suppose you were a Sunday School teacher and one lesson passage you were to teach is John 4:1–28 (the story of Jesus and the woman at the well). Identify several specific things you would seek to help your class members learn and determine the appropriate level of learning for each of these things you want them to learn.

3. Make written notes on several things in this chapter which you would like to remember. Using the review plan described in this chapter, set up and follow a systematic schedule for reviewing this material.

GROUP DISCUSSION STARTERS

1. What are several personal skills which every intelligent adult should possess or seek to develop?

2. What are the five steps in problem solving? What are the advantages in spending time identifying and writing out the specific problem?

3. What are some of the personal goals which motivate most adults to learn?

4. Select several major points in this chapter and discuss practical ways you can use this information.

NOTES

1. Bugelski, B. R., *The Psychology of Learning* (New York: Holt, Rinehart, and Winston, 1956), p. 8.

2. *Powerful Tools of Learning*, Chapter 1, pages 7–8 (Copyrighted by the Union College Character Research Project, Schenectady, N. Y., 1958).

3. Thomas F. Staton, *How to Instruct Successfully* (New York: McGraw-Hill Book Company, 1960), pp. 11–12.

4. *Powerful Tools of Learning*, p. 45.

CHAPTER 4
Reading to Remember

Thoughtful people through the centuries have recognized the relationship of reading to learning. Some of the most highly educated people of our day had only limited opportunities for formal schooling. Yet through avid reading they have become authorities in philosophy, the physical sciences, business administration, the fine arts, or other areas of human concern.

Countless thousands of other persons, although not recognized authorities in any field, have grown significantly as a result of their reading. From printed pages they have gained understandings and insights which have made life infinitely more useful to their families, their churches, and their communities.

But not all reading results in constructive learning. Postal authorities estimate conservatively that at least one hundred million brochures and catalogs offering obscene pictures and reading material are mailed each year. One's imagination is staggered by the thought of the billions of hours Americans spend annually reading the filthy literature offered in these brochures and catalogs. Not only are the minds contaminated but lives are marred. Police records indicate an appalling number of sex offences and other heinous crimes committed each year by persons who were motivated to their sinister acts by pornographic literature.

Thus if reading results in constructive learning, the reader must show discernment both in what he reads and in how he reads it.

In this chapter we shall explore five guidelines to constructive reading. As we consider each, analyze your own reading habits and plan ways to increase your learning through wholesome reading.

The five guidelines we shall consider are: (1) plan your reading; (2) set the stage; (3) preview the material; (4) gauge your speed; and (5) conserve the results.

Now let us consider individually each of these principles.

Plan Your Reading

A good reading program is never a haphazard, impulsive activity. The reader needs to plan his reading program as carefully as a good cook plans a menu.

Three purposes motivate most of our reading. They are pleasure, problem solving, and personal development. A person who is serious in his intent to increase his learning through a systematic reading program should include in that program a balance of each of these types of reading.

1. Reading for Pleasure

The serious reader recognizes the value of occasional reading for sheer relaxation and pleasure. A good book can quickly carry one's mind from the pressures and tensions of his daily routine to exciting adventure in faraway places. In planning a reading program, it is advisable to include reading for sheer entertainment.

The Reader's Digest and *The National Geographic Magazine* are classic popular magazines filled with interesting, highly readable articles. In addition to providing hours, or brief moments, of pleasure reading many of the articles and special features in these magazines make excellent conversational topics.

In selecting novels, many intelligent readers enjoy reading consecutively several books by the same author. The works of Ernest Hemingway or Thomas Wolfe, for example, are invitations to many hours of relaxing and highly entertaining reading.

2. Reading to Solve Problems

But one who wants to continue his education through reading does not spend all of his leisuretime reading for entertainment. His purposes are far more serious and call for reading materials which also "stretch the mind." Thus another purpose which motivates reading is the desire to find answers to specific personal problems.

Life is filled with problems. No one is immune to them. There are big problems and little problems, problems which disturb sleep and problems which deplete the pocketbook, problems which other persons know about and problems known only to oneself.

Stop reading for a moment and think of five personal problems you are facing now. Has this month outlived your last pay check? Is the carburetor on your car "acting up" again? Is your wife after you, whose ignorance about carpentry would fill a book, to build a cabinet for the utility room? Is the baby causing trouble by thumb-sucking, bed-wetting, or temper tantrums? Are you facing problems in your work? your family? your church? your community?

Somewhere, perhaps within a mile of you right now, there may be books and magazines dealing specifically with each problem you are facing. Where to find them? That's the thrill and the value of planning a reading program which deals directly with life's inevitable problems.

Of course, the public library is one of the likely sources for finding written help on your problems. Librarians and their assistants usually provide excellent assistance in locating resources dealing with specific problems. Except in emergencies, however, many people prefer to use the card catalog and *The Reader's Guide to Periodical Literature* in locating their own resources.

3. *Reading for Personal Development.*

A person serious in his desire to increase learning through reading will spend much time in reading for personal development.

Much of this reading will deal with current events. Our world is changing so rapidly that one must work hard to keep abreast. Two of the best sources of information on current events are newspapers and news magazines.

Much of a person's reading program needs to be related to vocational interests and responsibilities. In our day of social and technological changes, few, if any, jobs are remaining static. The opportunities and responsibilities of a position change as the world around it changes. As Alice in Wonderland discovered, one must run hard even to stay where he is. To advance in one's vocation, it is even more urgent that he continue to read and study. Trade journals, professional journals, and books all offer opportunities to keep abreast with what is going on in the area of one's vocational responsibility.

Avocational interests should also receive attention in a serious reading program. Poor indeed is the person who has no interests outside himself, his family, and his work. The world is filled with interesting people and areas of human concern. The serious reader selects one or more areas as centers of interest in his reading program.

Possibilities are virtually limitless. To mention only a few, there are people who helped shape history, automation and its influence upon our daily lives, communication skills, civil disobedience and race riots, Indians in America, and even that proverbial topic of conversation —the weather. Each of these areas offers possibilities of hours of pleasant and profitable reading.

Reading, properly planned and pursued, can also be an important factor in one's spiritual growth. The chief resource for this kind of reading, of course, is the Bible itself. In addition to the Bible, there are many other books which offer possibilities for spiritual development. A classic in the devotional field is John Baillie's *A Diary of Private Prayer*. Of a different nature but equally good is *God Being My Helper* by Ralph Herring.

The main thing is to plan your reading. Do not leave it to chance or impulse. Anyone who does not have at least one good book he is reading at all times is not likely to be a serious reader. It is preferable to have two or more books in the process of being read at all times. In this way, it is possible to select the reading to fit one's mood.

Set the Stage

Physical surroundings significantly affect the quality of learning a person gains from reading. Select as a regular location for your reading a good place where you will be as free as possible of interruptions and disturbances. Encourage your family to cooperate by not interrupting you unnecessarily while you are reading.

A comfortable chair and a good light are musts. Too little or too much light causes eye strain, which impedes reading and causes one to tire easily. For maximum ease in reading, the light should come over the reader's shoulder rather than being directly overhead or on the other side of the page from the reader.

Although comfort is important, too much comfort may impede reading. Generally speaking, except possibly for light reading, it is unwise to lie down to read.

Accumulate all of the materials you need before you begin your reading. If you plan (or need) to take notes on your reading, be sure to get note material and pencils before you begin to read. It is a good idea, also, to have a dictionary nearby.

Time is another important factor in reading for results. Some people are able to read far into the night, seemingly with power of concentration. Others find it better to schedule serious reading either during the day or the early evening. Regardless of when you read, remember that the Army plan of drilling for fifty minutes and taking a ten-minute rest is also a good schedule for the serious reader to follow.

Preview the Material

A prominent speaker, when asked the secret of his effectiveness, replied, "I tell them what I'm going to tell them. I tell them. Then I tell them what I told them." This pattern of preview, exploration, and review is also an effective plan to follow in reading.

Previewing a book, magazine, or newspaper before reading it can help one in several ways. First, it gives a broad overview of that which one will read later for details. Also, it helps the reader acquire certain "mental pegs" on which to "hang" information gained through the more careful reading. Previewing helps one acquire a background understanding which makes possible a better understanding of that which he will read. Finally, previewing, especially of a book, helps the reader to determine something of the style of the writer and the mood of the material to be read.

In previewing a book, it is wise to look first at the title page. Note the title, author, and publisher. Each of these is a clue to what the book is likely to be. Read the preface and other introductory material before looking at the contents page. The contents page, of course, provides the best clue to the contents of the book.

The procedure for previewing a newspaper or a magazine are similar. Scan the newspaper, especially the front page, or the table of contents page of a magazine to identify the articles which seem to be most interesting and significant to you. In this scanning, get a general idea of the articles to come back and read more carefully.

Frequently, one has only a limited time for reading a newspaper. It is good, therefore, to understand the anatomy of a news story. Usually, the writer answers in early paragraphs the questions what, who, when, and where. Other details, such as why, are given later in the body of the news story.

Out of the preview of the book, magazine, or newspaper, there should come one or more specific purposes for further reading. Spache and Berg stress the importance of this purpose in their observation, "When we have a clear-cut, detailed purpose, we will read with good concentration and understanding. When we are not sure exactly why we are reading, we read in a disorganized and desultory manner and remember little." [1]

Gauge Your Speed

Some people erroneously assume that speed is a characteristic of all good readers. While it is true that most good readers are capable of reading rapidly, not all materials should be read rapidly. The nature of the material should determine the speed of reading.

"The ability to read at widely different rates, chosen deliberately according to the purpose of the reading," observe Spache and Berg, "is one of the outstanding characteristics of a truly effective reader." [2]

The good reader is able to read material of average difficulty at a rate of approximately 250 to 350 words per minute. Difficult, technical material may slow him down to from 100 to 200 words per minute. On the other hand, if reading light material for sheer entertainment, he may be able to accelerate his speed to from 400 to 500 words per minute. The good reader recognizes the need for flexibility in speed, and deliberately decelerates or accelerates his speed when the nature of the material demands slowing down or speeding up.

Conserve the Results

Nothing is a greater waste of time than sitting, book in hand, looking idly into space. Of little more value is scanning lines of print without comprehending their meaning. Learning results from reading only when there is some comprehension of the meanings communicated by the type.

The first step in comprehending these meanings is to concentrate on that which is being read. Earlier we saw that moderate concentration may result in some learning but intense concentration causes the learning to increase sharply.

Many people falsely assume that one has to be "in the mood"' to read before he can get anything from reading. This is not true. By reading, one can create a mood for further reading. The person who is dependent upon "moods" to do something seldom accomplishes anything. Thomas Huxley said that a fundamental purpose of education is to teach students that the most valuable trait they can acquire is "the ability to make yourself do the thing you have to do, when it ought to be done, whether you like it or not."

Certain supplementary techniques can help you "get into" your reading. One of these techniques is to offer rewards. For example, promise yourself that if you will concentrate diligently on a book for fifty minutes, you will stop long enough to eat an apple. This little technique provides additional incentive for concentration.

Perhaps the best technique for helping one to concentrate is to raise certain questions about the material to be read. Reading then has purpose—finding answers to those questions. One value of previewing material before it is read is that one can identify relevant questions, the answers of which may be found during the more careful reading.

Note-taking is another technique which helps the reader conserve the results of his reading. The writer uses stenographic notebooks for this purpose. On the outside cover, he keeps a record of the dates the first and the last notes in the notebook were made. The pages of the pad are numbered consecutively. On the inside front cover, he keeps a record of the books read and the page numbers on which the corresponding notes appear. Reading notes are kept on one side of the pages only. The reverse side of each page is reserved for ideas which come during the reading—ways the material can be used or related ideas which call for further study. The shorthand pads fit easily into a bookshelf, where they are available for quick reference.

The review is another technique for remembering that which has been read. Research reveals that we forget most of what we learn within forty-eight hours of the time we learn it. However, recall does increase memory. It is good, therefore, to review one's reading notes periodically. These periodic reviews greatly increase permanent learnings.

Of course, the best way to conserve the results of reading is to use as soon as possible and as often as possible that which was read. If no other use is available, simply discussing what has been read with a friend or family member can be a helpful factor in remembering.

PERSONAL LEARNING ACTIVITIES

1. List the titles of the books you have read during the past month. Does the number and the type of books you have read indicate that you are seriously interested in increasing your learning through reading? Select a goal of the number of books to read during the next month. Select the books and work out a reading schedule.

2. Select a copy of a current newsmagazine to read. Preview the magazine first, and identify several questions for which you want to find answers as you read the magazine. Make notes on information to remember.

3. Select a problem you are facing and seek to read material dealing with that problem.

GROUP DISCUSSION STARTERS

1. How much time should an intelligent adult spend during an average week in reading books, magazines, and the newspaper?

2. What are the two best newsmagazines available today? Why do you consider them to be best?

3. What are some good techniques for remembering what you read?

NOTES

1. George D. Spache and Paul C. Berg, *The Art of Efficient Reading* (New York: The Macmillan Company, 1955), p. 13.
2. *Ibid*, p. 16.

CHAPTER 5
Listening to Learn

Several years ago parents all over America became excited over a book entitled *Why Johnny Can't Read*. In this book, the author, Rudolph Flesch, made a sweeping indictment against methods public schools use to teach reading. As a result, he charged, the average child in public school simply does not learn to read effectively.

Although Flesch's indictment may or may not be valid, thoughtful people should be greatly concerned over the inability of Johnny and his parents to listen. For poor listening is perhaps the number one reason most of us gain so little from the scores of valuable learning opportunities we have each day.

The average person, according to research findings of Nichols and Stephens,[1] listens at approximately a 25 percent level of efficiency. Ironically, more than one half the time we spend in verbal communication is spent in listening. In careful research, Paul T. Rankin discovered that his subjects spent an average of 70 percent of their time each day in verbal communication. Nine percent of this time was spent in writing. Sixteen percent was spent in reading. Thirty percent was spent in talking. Forty-five percent was spent in listening.

Probably one reason we are such poor listeners is that listening, as important as it is, has never been given its rightful place among the "three r's" in our school curricula. Rankin also discovered that the Detroit school system placed 52 percent of the emphasis in classroom instruction on reading, while listening received only 8 percent. As recently as 1958, textbooks used in graduate courses on research in the teaching of the language arts described such courses as reading, writing, speaking, and spelling. No reference was made to listening.[2]

Thus most of us are poor listeners simply because we have never considered good listening to be a necessary part of our everyday life.

Some False Assumptions About Listening

Before we can become good listeners, we must overcome several false assumptions about listening. Some of these false assumptions are the following:

1. Listening ability depends largely upon intelligence.

Although many persons of high intelligence have taught themselves to listen effectively, there is no direct relationship between listening and intelligence. A person with average, even slightly below average, intelligence who listens carefully may learn more than a person of high intelligence who is a poor listener. Good listening does not depend upon exceptional intelligence.

2. *Special training is not necessary for one to become a good listener.*

The actions of most of us suggests that we feel that special training in listening is unnecessary. Yet our listening efficiency level of 25 percent suggests that we desperately need special training in listening. Later in this chapter, we shall consider some of the methods one can use to improve his listening skill.

3. *Listening skill is closely related to hearing acuity.*

Many people have never stopped to recognize the vast difference between hearing and listening. Hearing is the physical ability to detect, through the stimulation of auditory nerves in the ear, sound waves. Listening implies a conscious effort to interpret meanings being communicated through those sounds. Thus, although hearing and listening are closely related, they are by no means the same thing.

4. *The main objective of listening is to "get the facts."*

Some people assume that good listening is simply understanding and remembering each individual fact spoken by the speaker. Although listening does imply an understanding and retention of certain facts, good listening is far more than simply memorizing facts spoken. Actually, an effort to remember each fact in the order spoken may keep one from comprehending the basic ideas and meanings being communicated. Thus, listening is more than simply "getting the facts."

Obstacles to Listening

In addition to these false assumptions, which themselves constitute barriers, there are several formidable obstacles to good listening.

1. Lack of Motivation

One of the greatest obstacles to listening is lack of motivation. We don't listen simply because we do not make a conscious effort to understand.

2. Preoccupation

The wandering mind frequently leaves one wondering what was said. This is especially true in listening to a sermon or public address. One speaker commended a woman for her attentiveness during a speech he had just made. "Oh," replied the woman, "I'm afraid I didn't hear all you said, but my mother taught me always to have a 'listening face.'"

3. Ease of Distraction

Many people allow the physical appearance of the speaker, his voice or mannerisms, or other movement or noise in the room to distract them from listening. The good listener disciplines himself to ignore visual and auditory distractions and to concentrate on the meanings the speaker is seeking to communicate.

4. Aversion to Difficult Listening

Many of us are simply averse to trying to listen to anything which is difficult to comprehend. When the content of a speech or sermon is difficult, we relapse into our own little world with the smug excuse that "it's just over my head."

5. Emotional Filters

Perhaps the greatest obstacle to effective listening is a tendency on the part of most of us to hear what we want to hear and to "filter out" things which are unpleasant to us. All of us are familiar with the saying that in the eyes of a mother her son can do no wrong. Because of her great love for him she "hears" only that which is good about him. Other things she "filters out" because they are inconsistent with the concept she has of her son. There is a tendency on the part of all of us not to hear good things about persons we dislike and to "hear" only good things about persons we like.

Emotional filters create problems in listening for most of us. We need to make a deliberate effort to discover where these filters are operative in our own experience. When we discover these, we need to analyze our attitude toward the object of this filter and make a deliberate effort to remove the filter. Effective listening is objective; we cannot listen effectively if emotional filters are creating biases.

Ways to Improve Listening

Anyone who is serious in his desire to improve his listening ability can learn to do so. Good listening is a skill. Like any other skill, it does not develop automatically as a part of the maturation process. It must be cultivated.

One of the first steps in becoming a good listener is to recognize the different types of listening situations. Sometimes we listen during a conversational dialogue. This happens when we are talking freely with one or more other persons. On other occasions, we listen during an informal discourse. This happens when one person is speaking to us and we are replying only infrequently. A third type of listening is that which is done during a sermon or other public address.

There are some general principles which apply in all types of listening situations. Other principles apply primarily (although not exclusively) to each respective type of listening situation.

One general principle is to listen for use. As you listen, continue to ask yourself questions concerning the value of what is being said to you personally. How can I use what is being said? What can I do during the next few days actually to put into practice some of the things being said? Listening for use is one of the best ways to improve one's listening skill.

Another general principle is to listen for *essential* facts or details. Most speakers include in their discourse certain facts which are essential to an understanding of what they are saying and other facts which either support or make more interesting these essential facts. It is well, therefore, to raise in your mind questions and to listen for answers to such questions as those which structure a newspaper story—who? what? when? where? and why? It is unlikely that the speaker will organize his discourse neatly around these questions, but a skilful listener will be alert to detect answers to these and other relevant questions as they are given.

It is also good to listen for the basic principle or issue underlying the essential facts being discussed. Many times the basic issue will not be stated explicitly. The speaker himself may not be aware of the basic issue, and the facts he gives may not be the real cause of the problem he is discussing. The intelligent listener seeks to listen "beneath the surface" of what is being said to discover the real issue.

Finally, in all listening experiences it is well to "listen" for nonverbal clues. These may be facial expressions, the tone of voice or pauses in speech, even the speaker's physical posture. Through these nonverbal expressions, the good listener may be able to detect apprehension, fear, suspicion, frustration, or deep satisfaction. Many times these nonverbal clues are far more important to an understanding of what the speaker is saying than are the words he uses.

Let's consider now some specific types of listening.

1. Conversational Dialogue

A common fault of most of us is that we do not listen carefully when we are engaged in a personal conversation. This is especially true if the conversation is of a controversial nature. We become so concerned with what we will say next that we actually fail to hear what the other person is saying. Consequently, we reply not to what was said but to what we think was being said or what might have been said earlier. It has been suggested that persons involved in a controversial discussion might well agree that each would repeat what the other person has said before attempting to reply. This would slow down the discussion and improve communication.

Even if this is not done, a good listener listens carefully to all that is being said during a conversational dialogue. If the other person "gets off the track" of the main topic, he may tactfully direct the conversation back to the main issue. However, he is alert to what was said during these digressions. Many times they are significant clues to the speaker's attitude toward the topic under discussion.

2. Informal Discourse

All of us find ourselves occasionally listening as someone else tells of a personal experience or talks about something else. For many people, this is the most difficult type of listening. The reason for this difficulty is the vast difference in our rate of thinking and the rate the other person speaks. We think at a rate of approximately 500 words per minute. The average person speaks at a rate of approximately 150 or 200 words per minute. Thus we have to slow down our thought processes to the rate of someone else's speech. Many times, as a result, we listen for awhile and then let our minds wander. Suddenly, we jerk our minds back and listen some more, only to find, after a few minutes, the same temptation to let the mind wander off again.

Nichols and Stephens [3] made a study of a number of good listeners to discover how they listen during informal discourses. They discovered several things which can be of help to us.

Good listeners, they discovered, think ahead of the speaker, trying to guess what he is leading up to, what conclusions will be drawn from what is being said.

Good listeners also weigh the verbal evidence the speaker is using to support the points he is making.

Good listeners periodically review what has been said up to that point.

Finally, good listeners, they discovered, "listen between the lines" in search of meanings not verbalized.

These techniques can be of great help to us in improving our listening during a conversational monologue or during a public address.

3. Public Address

How many hours during the past month have you spent listening to a public speaker? How much do you remember about what was said? Perhaps you do not remember a great deal of what you heard.

The reason for this is that most of us are notorious listeners to public speakers. We listen for awhile, and then allow our minds to wander to another topic.

Frequently, the problem is not in the lack of intrinsic interest in what is being said. The real problem is our inability to concentrate for a sustained period and listen to a public address.

If we are serious in our desire to increase learning by listening more intelligently, we probably need to work hard at the task of improving our listening to public addresses. One of the best ways we can do this is to recognize the pattern or outline of what is being said, and organize what we hear around this pattern or outline.

Many centuries ago Greek and Roman orators developed a pattern for their oral discourses. That pattern continues to be followed by most speakers today.

The first step in that pattern is an introduction. Through a striking statement, an interesting anecdote, or some other interest-catching method, the speaker tries to get the attention of his audience. His introduction may or may not be directly related to what will be said in the main part of the discourse. Therefore, the listener needs to interpret the introduction in the light of what the speaker is attempting to do—attract the attention of his audience.

Following the introduction is a thesis of the address. In one sentence or many sentences, the speaker states the theme of his address. The listener needs to be extremely careful to catch the main points the speaker makes in developing his thesis.

Finally, the speaker concludes his address, usually by drawing a logical deduction, summarizing, or suggesting a possible course of action in the light of what he has said.

After all is said and done, good listening calls for rigid personal discipline. The techniques discussed in this chapter can be helpful, but a person must apply himself diligently if he uses them effectively.

We must learn to listen if we listen to learn.

PERSONAL LEARNING ACTIVITIES

1. Take careful notes of the next sermon or other public address you hear. Record the main thesis of the message, the points made to support the thesis, and the conclusion reached.

2. See if you can identify several "emotional filters" which impede your listening. Analyze each to see if you can discover the reason you have each of the "filters." How can you remove each one?

3. As you listen to various persons speak, see what "non-verbal" clues you can detect?

4. The next time you hear someone speak at length in an informal or formal discourse, do the following things: (1) think ahead of the speaker, trying to guess what he is leading up to; (2) weigh the verbal evidence he is using to support each point; (3) periodically review what he is saying; and (4) "listen between the lines" in search of meanings not verbalized.

GROUP DISCUSSION STARTERS

1. Why is it important for a person to be able to listen? skilfully?

2. Why is the average adult a poor listener?

3. How can one improve his listening ability?

NOTES

1. Ralph G. Nichols and Leonard Stevens, *Are You Listening?* (New York: McGraw-Hill Co., 1957), p. 6.

2. Gloria L. Horrworth, "Listening: A Facet of Oral Language," *Elementary English,* December, 1966, pp. 856–864.

3. Nichols and Stevens, *op. cit.,* pp. 81–82.

CHAPTER 6
Every Man My Teacher

On one occasion Gaines S. Dobbins asked William Lyon Phelps the secret of his freshness and vitality. Dr. Phelps, who then was approaching his eightieth birthday, replied: "If I have a secret, it is this: I have never met a person who was not interesting." [1]

Each person we meet can be our teacher, for each one possesses something interesting which can enrich our lives. If we open our eyes and overcome our biases, we may discover that we can learn much even from persons whom we consider unattractive or boring.

Some of life's most valuable lessons are learned from other people. These lessons are learned from people who have faced the same problems we face, or who have experienced the frustrations we experience. As we see how they deal with life's inevitable problems or frustrations, or as we listen to what they have to say, we learn some of our most valuable lessons about life itself.

The pages of history likewise are filled with records of persons whose lives even yet can enrich our lives. For the problems we face are not new to our generation. Our basic problems, such as fear, anxiety, frustration, suffering, and personal loss, have been the experiences of men and women through the centuries.

Let's consider some examples of the lessons we can learn from other persons from the past and present. The experiences or viewpoints of some of the persons we will consider may not be the ones for which these persons are best known. If this be so, it simply bears out the truth that little known facts about some people may be the things about them which can help us most.

Learning to Overcome Defeat

A graduate student in a Southern school had worked several years for a doctor's degree. His family had sacrificed heroically in order that he might remain in school. At long last he completed all of his requirements for the degree except the final oral examination. So certain was he that he would pass the examination successfully that he accepted an excellent position in a distant city.

The examination proved to be more difficult than he had anticipated. Despite his diligent preparation, he did not pass. The disappointment was bitter. The embarrassment was almost more than he could stand.

For several days he was almost overcome with remorse and self-pity. Finally, the thought came to him that his remorse and self-pity were only making matters worse for him and for his family. Although he had failed, life must go on.

With this in mind, he sat down and wrote to each member of his faculty examining committee. He thanked them individually for failing him inasmuch as, in their opinions, he was not qualified to pass. He asked for permission to study for another year and then to take the examination again.

A year later he took the examination and passed with flying colors. Faculty members and administrative personnel were so impressed by the character traits he had displayed that he was invited to remain as assistant to the president of his school.

Another young man put all of his savings into a partnership in a store. Bankruptcy necessitated the closing of the store with the loss of every cent of his investment. Undaunted, he entered partnership with a friend in another store. Within a few months, due to the insobriety of his partner, his second business venture failed and left him a crushing debt.

Still determined, he obtained work as a surveyor, borrowing money to purchase surveying equipment. Before he could begin work, creditors took the instruments to apply on his debts. About this time he suffered the greatest tragedy of his life—the death of his wife.

This fourth loss was almost more than he could bear.

His health broke, and he had to spend several months recuperating in the home of his parents.

When he recovered, he resolved to make a comeback. This time he decided to enter politics. He ran for and was elected to Congress. After his first term his constituents refused to reelect him. Twice thereafter he ran unsuccessfully for the Senate. Seven failures and a tragic loss, but he was still undefeated!

Two years after his second defeat for the Senate, he was chosen by his party to run for the presidency of the United States. He ran, was elected, and became one of the truly great leaders in the history of our country.

His name was Abraham Lincoln.[2]

We can learn many lessons from the lives of these two men. First, we can learn the value of not giving up when failure comes. In the agonizing hours and days following defeat, feelings of remorse are normal. But feelings of remorse are one thing; wallowing in self-pity and feeding on hostility are entirely different. Note that the young student was remorseful, but he actually thanked the members of his faculty examining council for failing him.

On the pathway to almost every worthwhile achievement have been days of bitter disappointment. It has been said that a man struggling for a great objective is like a blind man groping up a hill. He never knows how near he is to the top until he reaches it. Giving up may mean sitting down a few feet from the goal.

From the lives of these two men we also can learn that our reaction to defeat is far more important than the defeat itself. In the context of the student's whole life, the delay of one year in getting his doctorate was not a major factor—except that it gave the faculty and administration of his school an opportunity to see him demonstrate qualities of patience, humility, and perseverance. It was in his hour of defeat that his true character became known.

Finally, from the lives of these men we can learn that defeat often is simply a door closing to direct our lives into a more useful field of service. If Abraham Lincoln had succeeded in his early business ventures, he probably would be unknown in history today. It was closed doors in business that ultimately directed his life to the White House and into history.

Learning to Live One Day at a Time

Dr. William Osler was one of the truly great physicians of the past century. He was recognized, said Dr. Harvey Cushing, his biographer, as the most eminent and widely influential physician of his time.[3]

A Canadian by birth, Dr. Osler spent most of his professional career on the faculty of the Medical College of John Hopkins University. He is credited with being one of the four doctors who revolutionized medical education in the United States.

But in lay circles, Dr. Osler is perhaps remembered best for his famous essay, "A Way of Life." "Now the way of life I preach," wrote Dr. Osler, "is a habit to be acquired gradually by long and steady repetition. It is the practice of living for the day only, and for the day's work, *life in day-tight compartments*."

He encouraged his readers to let the limit of their horizons be a twenty-four hour circle. "The load of tomorrow, added to that of yesterday, carried today makes the strongest falter," he wrote.

Dr. Osler did recommend that a person carefully work out long range objectives. His own example, in addition to the admonition in his essay, attests the value of making careful plans for the future. But he stressed strongly the value of not worrying over past mistakes or becoming excessively concerned over things which might (or might not) happen in the future. Live "life in day-tight compartments" was his counsel to his readers then and to us today.

Learning to Deal with Problems

René Descartes was a French philosopher, mathematician, and soldier of the seventeenth century. He is well known for his basic assertion, "I think, therefore I am."

He is also well known for his four rules for straight thinking. One of those rules was to divide each problem into as many parts as possible and as might be necessary for its adequate solution.

Thus from Descartes we can gain valuable insight into a strategy for dealing with problems. If we follow his wise counsel, we will discover several things. Among them are the following:

1. We need to develop a strategy for dealing with problems. Most of us simply react to surface symptoms. We need to take positive action to deal intelligently with our real problems.

2. Most "problems" actually are composite of numerous closely related problems. We need to analyze the "problem" into its component parts and study interrelationships of these subsidiary problems.

3. Many times that which appears to be the problem is not the main problem at all. Only by "breaking" the problem into its parts can we discover the main problem and its interrelationships to surface symptoms.

4. Clear, analytical thinking and positive action are good anecdotes for emotionalism.

5. Problems are learning opportunities. Certain qualities, such as patience and self-control, are developed best by dealing constructively with problems.

Learning to Overcome Mistakes

"You Have a Right to your Misstakes!" was the title of an article appearing in an earlier issue of *Guideposts.*[4] The misspelled word "misstakes" was marked out by a line drawn through it and the proper spelling set above it.

In the article, the writer told of several persons who made serious mistakes, but who learned something from their mistakes. Winston Churchill was one of the persons about whom she wrote. She said:

On the international political scene, young Winston Churchill made so many outrageous errors that he was damned by the press for his "lack of discretion and judgement"—an indictment which, if he had allowed it to curtail his activities, would have robbed the Allies of a magnificent leader during the darkest years of World War II.

A Sunday School teacher of Junior boys went to her pastor in tears protesting the incorrigible behavior of Tom, a member of her class. Tom's latest antic was to jump out the window and throw rocks back into the classroom. In desperation, the teacher asserted that she would no longer teach the class if Tom were allowed to come back.

The wise pastor arranged to have Tom transferred to another class. Tom's new teacher, through loving understanding, won his confidence and affection. She also discovered, through visiting in his home, some things which helped to explain Tom's behavior.

When Tom's first teacher learned how the second teacher had won his confidence, she recognized her own mistakes in dealing with him. Over a period of months, through diligent effort, she changed her whole approach to teaching. Today she has the reputation of being one of the best children's workers in any church in her city.

And, incidentally, Tom today is a minister and prominent worker with boys.

Beth Day, in her article in *Guideposts*,[5] stresses the fact that mistakes are an acceptable part of life. They are essential, she says to a full life. Without the intelligent use of mistakes, we would never master anything. Yet some of us, she continues, are so burdened by the fear of making a mistake that we cheat ourselves out of the very thing we want most to do.

In the lives of Winston Churchill and the Sunday School teacher we find examples of persons who made mistakes, but who overcame their mistakes and became useful leaders. The Sunday School teacher says today that any success she has experienced is due largely to the lessons she learned from her mistakes in dealing with Tom.

Lessons from Life

From the lives of men and women cited in this chapter, we see that we can learn much from the experiences of other persons. But such learning is not accidental nor haphazard. As in any other kind of learning, there are steps in the learning process. This is not to say that we must consciously and deliberately follow in sequence each of these steps if we are to learn anything. It is to say, however, that we will learn more and faster if we discipline ourselves to follow these principles.

1. Develop a respect for the dignity of everyone.

The first step in learning from another person is to respect his dignity and worth. The Christian faith affirms the supreme value of every human being. Made in God's image, each person is of great value to the Creator and Sustainer of the universe. If he is valuable to God, he likewise should be a person of dignity and worth in our sight.

No person ever sinks so low that he does not have some good in him. There is in everyone some trait we would do well to emulate or some viewpoint we would do well to heed. It is true that we have to look and listen long and diligently to discover these traits and viewpoints in some persons. It also is true that we can learn more from some persons than we can from others. Yet we can learn something from everyone. Every man can be our teacher.

2. *Learn to discover and isolate desirable behavior patterns.*

If we would learn from another person, we need to discover and isolate the specific traits or viewpoints which we would learn. We may have high admiration for some person, but it is unlikely that we will pattern our actions after his until we discover what it is about him which we want to emulate. It may be his friendly disposition, his cheerfulness in the face of difficulties, or his ability to remain calm under pressure. Each of these actions reflects specific character traits which are not developed accidentally. If they are developed to any appreciable degree, they must first be identified and analyzed and we must consciously seek to develop them.

3. *Practice new patterns of behavior.*

Trial and error is a familiar method of learning. No one expects to develop manual skills automatically or instantaneously. In learning to ride a bicycle, for example, one tries, falls off, and tries again. This process is continued until finally the learner is able first to wobble along a few feet and, after many more falls, to ride easily.

Likewise in developing skills in personal behavior one must use the trial and error method. For example, one does not learn without effort to speak in an even, unemotional tone when someone else is shouting at him. He practices and through trial and error he develops this ability. Thus the trial and error method, well accepted in developing manual skills, must also be used in developing personal skills in other areas of life.

PERSONAL LEARNING ACTIVITIES

1. Read a biography of a person in history whom you admire. What traits did he possess which you would like to emulate? How can you develop those traits?

2. If you know someone who overcame serious disappointment or tragedy, talk with that person about his experience. Ask him what sustained him during his darkest hour. Ask, also, what lessons he learned from the experience.

3. Select a person whom you highly respect and analyze his personality to identify his traits which are responsible for your attitude toward him.

4. Select a person for whom you have little respect. Analyze his personality to discover two or three traits which are admirable.

5. Analyze your own personality to discover two or three weaknesses. Think of persons in your acquaintance who possess the traits which you need to develop to overcome your weaknesses. Try to emulate the persons who possess the traits which you need.

GROUP DISCUSSION STARTERS

1. Who are some people you have known who overcame serious problems or tragedies and went on to achieve happiness and usefulness? Tell about their experiences.

2. Who are some people who have exerted profound influence upon your life? What was it about them which caused them to have so much influence upon you?

3. In what sense can we learn more from people than we can learn from books?

NOTES

1. Gaines S. Dobbins, *Great Teachers Make a Difference* (Nashville: Broadman Press, 1965), p. 115.

2. Arno B. Reincke, "He Could Take It," *Readers' Digest,* February, 1963, pp. 140–142.

3. Moulton and Schiffers, *The Autobiography of Science* (Garden City: Doubleday, Doran, and Co., 1945), p. 605.

4. Beth Day, *Guideposts,* December, 1965, pp. 20–23.

5. *Ibid.*

CHAPTER 7
Learning Through Creative Thinking

Most people equate learning with gaining knowledge. Although acquiring knowledge is one important type of learning, we also learn in other ways. One other way is through creative thinking.

But, you may say, I just can't think creatively.

If you have at least average intelligence, you are wrong in that assumption. The late Alex F. Osborn, an outstanding authority in creativity, said:

Scientific tests for aptitudes have revealed the relative universality of creative potential. . . . An analysis of almost all of the psychological tests ever made point to the conclusion that creative talent is normally distributed in that *all* of us possess this talent to a lesser or greater degree—and that our creative efficacy varies more in ratio to our output of mental energy than in ratio to our inborn talents.[1]

Read again the last part of Dr. Osborn's statement. Our creative power, he says, is limited more by *our unwillingness to pay the price of creativity* than by our ability to be creative. This is a nice way of saying that laziness is one of our biggest obstacles to creative thinking.

If you knew for certain that laziness is keeping you from being a more creative person, would you resolve to do something about it? In this chapter you will find some scientifically proven principles for creative thinking. Through the use of these principles, you can become more creative—if you are willing to expend the energy!

But laziness is not the only obstacle many of us must overcome. Our formal schooling placed a far stronger emphasis on judicial thinking, or analyzing, comparing, and choosing, than on creative thinking, which visualizes, foresees, and generates ideas. Dr. Osborn states that over 90 percent of our schooling tends to train our judicial rather than our creative faculties. E. Paul Torrance, another authority on creativity, says that imagination tends to contract as knowledge expands.[2]

Other obstacles to creative thinking are timidity, emotional tension, and insensitivity to opportunities for creative thinking. Many of us are excessively dependent upon the thinking of other people. We are afraid to "stick our necks out" to do any of our own thinking. James Bryant Conant, while president of Harvard, kept on his office wall a drawing of a turtle with this caption: "Behold the turtle. He makes progress only when his neck is out."

Have you ever heard the expression "frozen stiff"? Although it may be an exaggeration, the emotions of fear, anxiety, and anger do tend to paralyze, rather than to free, creative processes.

In our age of tremendous technological advance it is ironical that many of us still are insensitive to opportunities for creative thinking. One man who had taken a course in creative thinking later told his instructor he had been fired from his job. When asked why, he answered: "I don't know. After taking your course, I was prepared all right. If they'd given me some problems to solve, I know I could have solved them. But they didn't give me problems. They just gave me a whale of a mess!" [3]

There are many forms of creative thinking. Each form has almost unlimited variations in procedure. It is impossible, therefore, to deal adequately in one chapter with the whole field of creative thinking. The best we can do is to identify and to explore an approach to two forms.

The forms we shall consider are creative problem solving and creative planning.

Creative Problem Solving

We all have in common at least one thing. We have problems. No one is immune to them. Even persons who seemingly are highly successful, who seem not to have a care in the world, frequently conceal behind a facade of success and prosperity, problems known only to themselves and perhaps a few close associates.

Problems may exist in any area of our lives. We are

subject to having personal problems, financial problems, workrelated problems, family problems, community problems, and church problems. For, you see, a problem is simply an obstacle in the pathway of an objective. We want something, but circumstances make it difficult or impossible for us to get what we want. The circumstances, or obstacles, then become our problem. As long as we have goals in life we will face obstacles and experience problems.

Unfortunately, many of us do not have an intelligent strategy for dealing with problems. We act as though ignoring the problem—or tearing into it broadside—will cause our problem to go away. Usually problems are not solved in this way.

Because problems are varied in nature, there is no single best plan for dealing with them. There are, however, a few steps which usually are effective. These steps were mentioned in Chapter 2. Let's consider them in greater detail now.

1. Identify and define the problem.

Strange as it may seem, many times we struggle to overcome the symptoms of a problem without actually knowing what the real problem is. This happens because many problems are complex in nature. Sometimes what we consider to be a problem is a combination of separate problems each of which affects the others. Occasionally, when we face a situation like this, the solving of the key problem relieves the tension and we are no longer bothered by the secondary problems. Thus the first step toward a solution is to find out what the real problem is.

On other occasions, we are faced with a complicated single problem which has many parts or expressions. To solve the problem, we must identify the crux of the problem and understand its several aspects or expressions.

Emotional reactions make problems more difficult to understand and to solve. Frequently our emotions latch onto a minor aspect of the problem, or even to something not at all related to the real problem. Thus when we get upset over something, it always is good to find out what actually has upset us before we take any action. Maybe we really are not upset over the basic problem, but, instead, over something only indirectly related to it.

Many times it helps to write down what we think to be the real problem and to list as many of its manifestations or parts as we can. The writing down of the problem begins to relieve some of the emotional tension and assures greater clarity of thought as we try to solve the problem.

2. Discover pertinent facts.

The second step in creative problem solving is to get the facts. To try to solve a problem without first getting all of the essential facts is like trying to build a house without having all of the essential material. Things just won't fit together very well.

Sometimes we have misinformation which seriously colors our thinking about the problem. Until we get the correct information we can never get a right perspective on the problem. Often we jump to conclusions on the basis of false information.

One approach to getting the facts is to ask what it is we want to do that we can't do because of the problem. What caused the problem to develop? Who was responsible? Was it intentional? Has a problem like this existed before? How was it overcome? Questions like these can help us to get information essential to a successful solution of the problem.

3. *Explore possible solutions.*

After securing the necessary facts, we are ready to explore possible solutions. Two things need to be kept in mind in this phase of problem solving. First, withhold judgment until you have had an opportunity to evaluate carefully all of the possible solutions. By jumping too quickly to a decision we close our minds to facts which might cause us to see the problem in a different light.

A second consideration is to identify as many possible solutions as you can think of. Research has proved conclusively that quality in creative thinking comes through the quantity of possible solutions considered. Thus we should identify and think through many possible solutions before attempting to select the right one.

4. *Determine the most plausible solution.*

After many possible solutions have been considered, we are in a better position to choose the most likely one.

This choice should be undertaken carefully and deliberately. One good approach is to list the advantages and disadvantages of each possible solution.

In an especially different situation, it also is wise, after advantages and disadvantages have been listed, to rank the advantages and the disadvantages in the order of their importance. Otherwise we may make a decision on the basis of a large number of weak advantages rather than a few strong disadvantages.

5. *Implement your decision.*

Once a decision is made, usually it is best to act upon it as quickly as possible. Delay may cause misgivings to arise. The enthusiasm which usually accompanies the solution of a problem may begin to wane. The circumstances surrounding the problem may change, and the solution may not be appropriate after a delay.

There is an old expression that impression without expression leads to depression. This is a good principle to keep in mind when a solution to a problem has been found.

Creative Planning

A second form of creative thinking is the process of creative planning. This type of creativity is achieved when one plans or performs a difficult task which requires visualizing, analyzing, exploring, assessing, and organizing.

One example of creative planning is the preparation of a speech. One may have in mind all, or almost all, of the facts and ideas to be used in the speech before beginning formal preparation. However, the process of selecting and organizing these facts and ideas around a new framework calls for creative action. The more one is forced to search through many sources for information and ideas to use and the harder he struggles to organize the facts and ideas into a new structure the greater the creative output.

There are at least four stages in creative planning. They might be described as the stages of perspiration, frustration, inspiration, and consolidation.[4]

The stage of perspiration.—Creative planning is hard work. One reason many people fail to plan creatively is that they short-cut the preparation, or perspiration, process. As Herbert Spencer once said, "Early ideas are not usually true ideas." There is the necessity to work hard, to explore, to analyze, to struggle, if our efforts are to result in true creative thinking.

One of the best ways to begin the process of creative planning is to clarify the specific objective. If the objective is to plan a speech, what is the exact topic or purpose. If the objective is to write an article, or to plan a homecoming parade, or to draw a diagram of your dream house, exactly what is it you are trying to do and why?

Next, before consulting outside sources, think through all of the information and ideas you have on the subject. Many times in your own experience you will have valuable information and ideas which can be used in creative planning.

Although it is good to begin with one's own information and ideas, seldom is it wise to limit this first phase to knowledge and ideas possessed. The next step is to investigate other sources. One's own books, the public library, other community resources, persons experienced in the area in which you are planning, and all other available sources of pertinent information should be consulted.

After collecting a wealth of information and ideas, far more than can possibly be used, begin to try to formulate your own plans. This phase of planning has been called the period of "false starts." If you reach the point of real creativity, it is essential that you first make many attempts which seem to be completely fruitless. Depending upon the size of the project, many hours, or days, may be spent gathering information and ideas and making "false starts."

The stage of frustration.—After the exhaustive search for ideas and information and a series of what may seem to be endless "false starts," frustration usually sets in. There is the feeling that time has been completely wasted and all the material gathered should be disposed of immediately. Usually the harder one has worked, or the stronger the desire to do a good job, the keener the frustration. When this frustration comes, do not do anything desperate. Frustration is par for the course at this point. Actually, intelligent frustration is creativity in embryonic form.

In this period of frustration, often approaching desperation, it can be comforting to know that this same frustration is a common experience to persons known to be outstanding creators. Hutchinson says:

It is a common conceit of intuitive thinkers to wish the public to believe that they proceed with immediate effectiveness to their work. They are in fact ashamed to let folk peep through the keyhole into their studies and laboratories. The chaos and confusion would be disillusioning. The piles of notes on odd bits of paper, the rejected pages of manuscripts or score sheet, the waste basket full of half-matured plans, the exasperation of style—all these evidences of indecisive thought would come into view, and reputations for efficiency, for creative maturity would straightway crumble.[5]

Once progress toward creative work is lost and frustration begins to mount, there is no sure way to recovery except a change of pace and rest. Try to forget the project entirely. A game of golf or some other physical exercise is especially helpful. Do anything to get away from your work, and try to forget it entirely.

The important thing is not to despair over the frustration. Recognize it as a normal experience, actually essential to true creativity.

The stage of inspiration.—By pulling away from the work and worry, the subconscious mind has an opportunity to begin to function. It is able to sort out ideas, to set things in proper relationships, to perceive heretofore unthought of possibilities. Suddenly, things begin to fall into place. Ideas come as flashes of insight. Many times an entire outline or broad structure will come suddenly into one's mind.

The period of inspiration is exciting. Whereas during the period of frustration the well of ideas seemed completely dry, during the period of inspiration ideas flood rapidly into the mind.

Although it may seem at the moment that the ideas are so strong that they will never be forgotten, it is a good idea to write them down. The moment of inspiration will pass. The time will come to get back to the drudgery of working out the details. Unless the ideas which flooded the mind during the period of inspiration are written down, they well may be forgotten when you get ready to use them.

The stage of consolidation.—The moment of insight is merely the beginning point of the final work of creative planning. When flashes of insight are coming, it is no time for critical thinking. To attempt to be judgmental may slow down the creative powers. Thus there is the need later to think through carefully, in the light of objective reality, the feasibility of the ideas which came.

There also is the need to select from the information and ideas which came during the period of perspiration those which are needed to support or to implement the central idea which came during the moment of creativity.

A final step is the refinement of the total outline or structure. Here major attention is given to the form or plans for presentation.

Thus we see the cycle of creative planning: perspiration, frustration, inspiration, and consolidation.

The process may be long and painful, but the reward is the satisfaction of true creativity.

PERSONAL LEARNING ACTIVITIES

1. Following the steps in creative problem solving, analyze a problem you are facing.

2. Select another problem and break it into as many subproblems as you can identify. Based on this analysis, define what you believe to be the main problem.

3. Select a project which can be accomplished through creative planning. As you work on the project, observe the four phases of perspiration, frustration, inspiration, and consolidation.

GROUP DISCUSSION STARTERS

1. Why do so few adults display evidences of real creativity?

2. Can a person increase his creativity? If he can, how? If he cannot, why not?

3. What are some common causes of frustration? Does frustration always lead to creativity? Why not?

4. What contribution is made by each of the steps in creative thinking?

5. What are some familiar activities which can be accomplished best through creative planning?

NOTES

1. Alex F. Osborn, *Applied Imagination* (New York: Chas. Scribner's Sons, 1953), p. 15.

2. *Ibid.*, p. 43.

3. *Ibid*, p. 87.

4. These steps are based on similar ones described in *How to Think Creatively* by Eliot Dole Hutchison (New York: Abingdon-Cokesbury Press, 1949).

5. *Ibid*, pp. 50–51.

CHAPTER 8
Learn More—Faster in Groups

We all have heard it said that a person is known by the company he keeps. It is equally true that a person learns *from* the company he keeps. Some of our most quickly acquired, most powerful, and longest remembered learnings are gained from association with other people.

Each of us is a part of many groups. They include our families, our colleagues at work, civic and fraternal organizations, church groups, and other clusters of persons. Through association with them, we acquire knowledge, formulate or change attitudes, and develop habits and skills. No consideration of adult learning opportunities would be complete without an exploration of opportunities for learning from the persons with whom we associate.

It is impossible in one chapter to explore learning opportunities with all of the groups of which we are a part.

Therefore, we will focus our attention on three types of groups. They are informal social groups, clubs and service organizations, and formal learning groups.

Informal Social Groups

During the early days following World War II, Walter, a German refugee, enrolled in a school in this country. He had few friends here and he spoke only broken English. But he had three assets which were tremendously valuable to him. He had a quick mind, a friendly disposition, and an enthusiastic interest in life.

Within one year Walter spoke flawless English, and he had become thoroughly Americanized. He understood our customs, and he could converse intelligently on a wide variety of subjects, such as sports, local politics, folk music, and regional cultural and social issues.

How had he learned so much in such a short period of time? Primarily through informal conversation with friends on the campus, at church, and in the community. Each time he heard an unfamiliar English word he asked its meaning. The word and its meaning were recorded in a small notebook which he kept in his shirt pocket. In another notebook he kept notes on other things of significance which he learned about American life. Through the company he kept, he learned, in a few short months, more about American life than many newcomers learn in several years.

Although Walter's experience may seem more dramatic than any we might have, we, too, can learn a great deal from persons with whom we associate. Each day we hear facts and attitudes expressed which can increase our store of knowledge and change our way of thinking. We observe behavior from which, if we are alert, we can learn important behavioral skills.

But if we would learn from the company we keep, we must follow Walter's example in at least two ways. First, we should try to associate with people who are well versed in the areas in which we would like to increase our learning. If we want to learn music, it makes good sense to associate with musicians. From their conversation, we can learn much about music.

We also should follow Walter's example in being alert for learning opportunities. He learned quickly because he wanted to learn, and he was constantly seeking to expand his store of knowledge.

Clubs and Service Organizations

Americans are notorious joiners. We join civic clubs, social clubs, professional clubs, avocational clubs, and many other kinds of organizations. Each of these offers its own special learning opportunities.

Civic clubs, such as Rotary International and the Kiwanis Club, in addition to providing stimulating "table talk," feature provocative speakers who talk on a wide range of topics. These addresses are learning opportunities *par excellence*.

Most cities or towns of any size have numerous special interest clubs. One young adult became a chess champion by joining a chess club and playing each Thursday evening. Millions of Ameican housewives have become experienced flower growers and floral designers by participating in garden clubs. The Farm Extension Bureau, through its various clubs and community activities, is one of the outstanding educational organizations in America. Music clubs, book clubs, the Parent Teachers' Association, and local political clubs offer additional learning opportunities.

Service organizations, although designed to help other people, offer their members special learning opportunities. Through participation in Gray Ladies, for example, hundreds of women have developed valuable skills in ministering to sick persons. Even raising funds for the Community Chest can help a person to develop skill in meeting people and in mobilizing people to meet human need.

Formal Learning Groups

A third invitation to learning comes from the informal and formal adult education classes in our churches and communities. Never have adult education courses been more accessible than they are today. Little attention has been given to them thus far, for the primary emphasis in this book is learning through informal, everyday experiences. However, we cannot consider continuing learning opportunities without considering formal classes or courses.

Everyone within the vicinity of a church has access to

group learning opportunities. The service of worship itself provides valuable opportunities to learn. Sunday School classes and other adult groups provide additional opportunities.

In most communities, the church is not the only institution or agency which provides group learning opportunities to adults. Public schools offer night classes for older learners. The Y.M.C.A., the Y.W.C.A., the Farm Extension Bureau, community colleges, and many other institutions provide courses for adults. If one is not familiar with adult learning opportunities in his community, a minister or the principal of the public school might be a valuable source of information about adult courses.

Assuming that the reader is familiar with available adult education classes in his community, indeed that he may already be enrolled in one or more courses, the main emphasis in the remainder of this chapter will be on ways to increase the quantity and the quality of learning in formal group situations.

When most of us were children, it was assumed that there were two primary ways of increasing learning in school. We could study hard and pay close attention to the teacher in class. Basic to this idea was the assumption that the teacher and the textbook were the sources of all knowledge to be communicated in the class. The teacher's chief objective was to transmit this learning to learners.

While the textbook and the teacher continue to be important resources in the learning process, most adult educators today reject a purely transmissive philosophy.

They believe that the group itself is a potent factor in the learning process. Seldom if ever is the teacher the only person in the class who has had past experience in the area being studied. Therefore, the past experiences of class members become important factors in the learning process. They share with one another their knowledge and viewpoints, and the teacher serves as a resource and a catalyst in stimulating and guiding learning in the class.

But this philosophy places upon the adult learner a responsibility many are unwilling to accept. This responsibility was described by Bergevin and McKinley: [1]

In the educational picture the trained leader, for example the teacher of the adult class, is too often forced to assume the full responsibility for the teaching-learning process. Participants expect him not only to teach them but to 'learn them' (learn for them). Part of this difficulty lies in the fact that we learners do not know how to participate responsibly. We therefore cannot accept the responsibility for actively helping ourselves, our fellow learners, and our leaders in a joint enterprise. We need to learn how to work with each other. We must become aware of actual ways in which we can help each other and our leaders. Then we must actually practice these skills, not merely have them pointed out.

What are some skills which need to be developed and practiced by adult learners in group learning situations?

1. Develop learning goals.

No discussion of skills for group learning would be complete without some attention to the significance of personal learning goals.

Bergevin and McKinley [2] points out: "If we are to learn most effectively, we adults must ourselves discover and recognize a personal reason for learning about a given topic. It is not enough for someone to tell us why he thinks it is important for us to learn a certain thing. We must *ourselves* recognize a personal reason."

Thus it is inadequate for an adult to say simply, "My goal is to take a course in woodwork." He needs to be more specific and say, for example, "I want to develop skill in using the band saw, the router, and the lathe." The course in woodwork then becomes a means of achieving his learning goal, not the goal itself.

All goals cannot be established at the beginning of a course. Although general goals can be established before the first session and clarified during early sessions, each session and each study assignment should be approached with a view to finding answers to specific problems rather than simply preparing an assignment or reading so many pages in a book.

2. *Learn to listen.*

In chapter 5, we explored ways to improve listening skills. Turn back and search the chapter for principles and techniques for improving listening in adult education classes.

Words are vehicles for communicating meanings. Often, in seeking to communicate meanings, speakers use words which mean to the listener something other than that which was intended to be communicated. Sometimes speakers use words incorrectly. Many speakers have difficulty organizing their thoughts with sufficient clarity to express the meanings they want to communicate.

Thus listening is more than patiently waiting until someone else finishes speaking. Good listening is an active process. It is a contemplation of the meaning of words and a decision as to the meaning the speaker intended the word to convey. It is a search beneath words for meanings which the speaker is trying to communicate. It is a hearing out of a speaker in an effort to understand fully what he is trying to say.

3. Don't chatter; say something.

An effective adult learner assumes responsibility for helping his group move toward its learning goals. There are several ways he can do this. One way is to raise questions when he feels that clarifications or additional information is needed. He also shares with the group his own understandings and experiences when those understandings and experiences can help the group move toward its goals. By proposing possible solutions to problems and helping evaluate possible solutions, the individual learner helps his learning group. A humorous remark sometimes can help relieve tension in a group. A cordial, personal comment at the beginning of a session may help the group establish rapport with one another.

Purposefulness in helping a group or class achieve its goals is the criterion by which we should measure all we say in an adult course. Humor for humor's sake may be a distracting influence; to relieve tension in order that the group may move toward its goals is a worthy objective.

4. Watch out for roadblocks.

Most adult learning groups occasionally encounter roadblocks. They reach the point where it seems they are not accomplishing anything, and they are unable to move forward or even to understand why they are stymied.

The responsible group member recognizes the roadblocks and seeks to discover their cause. Roadblocks may have several possible causes. Sometimes the group goal is unclear or group members are moving toward different goals. Sometimes inadequate information has been introduced into a group's thinking to solve the problem under discussion. Sometimes concealed hostility in the group impedes progress. Room conditions, such as stuffiness or outside distractions, may produce physical or emotional reactions which unconsciously block group progress.

The responsible group member is alert to roadblocks. When he detects a roadblock, he seeks to diagnose it and to use wise judgment in helping the group remove the block in order that the group may proceed toward its objectives.

5. Help with the housekeeping.

Housekeeping chores are not limited to the improvement of the physical appearance of a room or house. They also include certain functions which build relationships and cohesiveness among group members. Malcolm and

Hulda Knowles[3] have described six maintenance, or housekeeping, roles which group members may perform.

Encouraging—being friendly, warm, responsive to others, praising others and their ideas, agreeing with and accepting the contributions of others.

Mediating—harmonizing, conciliating differences in points of view, making compromises.

Gate keeping—trying to make it possible for another member to make a contribution by saying, "We haven't heard from Jim yet," or suggesting limited talking-time for everyone so that all will have a chance to be heard.

Standard setting—expressing standards for the group to use in choosing its subject matter or procedures, rules of conduct, ethical values.

Following—going along with the group, somewhat passively accepting the ideas or others, serving as an audience during the discussion, being a good listener.

Relieving tension—draining off negative feeling by jesting or throwing oil on troubled waters, diverting attention from unpleasant to pleasant matters.

A good group member becomes familiar with these housekeeping tasks and fills each from time to time.

6. *Be alert for hidden agenda.*

During recent years leaders in group work have been increasingly aware of the presence of hidden agenda in learning groups. By hidden agenda we mean the personal goals of group members which may not be known to the entire group.

Hidden agenda *per se* are neither good nor bad. One group member may have the hidden agenda to help a certain person in the group experience satisfaction and a feeling of meaningfulness in the group. He seeks to work on this in the group, but he works in such a way as not to be obvious. He has a hidden agenda, but that hidden agenda can help the group move toward its objectives.

Another person's hidden agenda may impede group progress. His agenda may be to discredit the teacher or leader or to guide the group to reach a conclusion or make a decision to his own personal interest. Concealed or hidden agenda like this do impede group progress. A responsible group member is ever alert to hidden agenda and uses good judgment, when such is discovered, to help the group cope with it.

PERSONAL LEARNING EXERCISE

To make this chapter more meaningful, why not take an inventory of your group learning opportunities? Make a list of the groups of which you are a part. Include informal and formal learning groups, clubs and service organizations, informal social groups, and any other group in which you participate.

Select from this list the five groups which, in your judgment, offer you the greatest learning potentials. Write out a list of things you have learned in each group during the past year.

Then make a list of learning goals you have as you participate in each of the five groups. Think through several approaches you can take in an effort to achieve each of these goals.

The rest is up to you.

GROUP DISCUSSION STARTERS

1. What kinds of roadblocks are encountered frequently in this group? How are they usually dealt with?

2. What are some of the common symptoms of hidden agenda? Under what circumstances is it best to expose hidden agenda? to leave it concealed?

3. What is the meaning of shared leadership in a group? Why is shared leadership better than having only one leader? Does shared leadership do away with the need for an appointed or elected leader? Why?

4. What do you consider to be the outstanding group learning opportunities in your community? Why? Why do so few adults take effective advantage of these opportunities?

NOTES

1. Paul Bergevin and John McKinley, *Design for Adult Education in the Church* (Greenwich: The Seabury Press, 1961), p. xx.

2. *Ibid.,* p. xviii.

3. Malcolm and Hulda Knowles, *Introduction to Group Dynamics* (New York: Association Press, 1959), pp. 52–53.

CHAPTER 9
Learning from Life's Inevitable Frustrations

Some of our most valuable learning opportunities come in the inevitable frustrations of life. Knowledge and understandings useful in many ways may be acquired as we face stark tragedy. Insights which change our entire outlook on life may be learned in an hour of crisis. Habit patterns which make life infinitely more meaningful may be developed during periods of severe physical or moral testing. Even learning simply to deal creatively with the frustration rather than being overcome by it is a valuable learning experience—one which probably could never be learned merely from a study of books.

A desire to learn is the secret. So long as we consider our troubles to be negative experiences from which no good can come, they are likely to be just that and nothing more. But no experience in life is ever so bad that we cannot learn something good from it. It is true that the good we learn from some experiences may be more than offset by the bad; but if we must experience the bad anyway, it makes good sense to gain from it anything we can. On other occasions, we can learn from our trials and tribulations lessons which far more than justify the suffering we endure.

Books may describe human experience, but they can never equate it. Many of life's most valuable lessons are learned in the crucible of life itself. Let us consider some of life's difficult experiences and some of the lessons we can learn while undergoing those experiences.

When Suffering Comes

The late Ellis A. Fuller, while pastor of a large church in a Southern city, had a simple but effective plan for visiting in the homes of all of his church members. His plan was to visit when one or more members of the family were experiencing suffering of some kind. In this way, he discovered, he would visit in each home sooner or later. He would visit most families sometime during the course of every year.

Dr. Fuller had learned that suffering is a universal experience. As one great Christian expressed it: "Suffering is so much the common experience of man that one can correctly say that to live is to suffer. . . . Suffering will join company with us if we walk long enough along life's highway. Sooner or later it will come and walk by our side." [1]

Persons experiencing suffering often ask two profound questions. What causes human suffering? How can I endure the suffering I am called upon to bear? Although profoundly significant, both of these questions are outside the scope of our immediate consideration. Anyone struggling with these two perplexing questions will find help in an intensely interesting little book entitled *Suffering: a Personal Perspective*. In this provocative book the author, T. B. Maston, reflects on some causes of human suffering and, out of his own personal experience, discusses ways to deal with it.

Our concern here is for lessons which can be learned from suffering. Some of the most valuable learning experiences of life come during dark hours of anguish and grief. But they do not come automatically. Two people may sustain identical losses. One of those persons may become embittered for life; the other may learn lessons which help him to live a richer, fuller life.

What are some of the lessons which can be learned from suffering? Let us consider three of them.

Patient perseverance is one of the lessons we can learn. Impatience is one of the characteristics of our culture. We want what we want when we want it. Suffering can help us learn to "hang on" long beyond the time it would be easier to give up. Patience and perseverance developed during a crisis can help us to meet other crises, small and great, throughout life.

Empathy is another lesson we can learn from suffering. Often it is said that we cannot fully sympathize with another person until we go through a similar experience. Suffering can give us understandings, insights, and a depth of feeling for others who are suffering.

Perhaps the outstanding lesson we can learn is the *reliability of spiritual resources*. Suffering often carries a person beyond the limits of his physical and emotional strength. At such times, many Christians recognize and claim strength not of themselves. Biblical promises, which previously may have been only words to them, were found to contain their only assurance and hope. Strength for any crisis can be found in God's promise that "my grace is sufficient for thee: for my strength is made perfect in weakness" (2 Cor. 12:9). When the reliability of such promises are tested and proven during crises, persons learn lessons which make them stronger and more useful to themselves and to others.

Act! Don't Just React

Several years ago a social scientist expounded what apparently he thought to be a new theory. He named it the social circular theory. There is a human tendency, he affirmed, for a person to react emotionally in terms of the same emotion expressed to him. If Joe expresses anger or bitterness toward Al, for example, Al tends to react in the same spirit of anger or bitterness toward Joe or to anyone else who might be around. To break the circuit, the social scientist affirmed, one needs to learn to act with a counter positive emotion rather than to react with a similar negative emotion.

Although the principal expounded in this theory is as sound as the law of gravitation, by no means is this a new theory. Another wise man centuries ago said, "A soft answer turneth away wrath: but grievous words stir up anger" (Prov. 15:1).

Unfortunately, many of us go through life without learning this lesson. If a person shouts at us, we shout back. When someone gets angry with us, this is sufficient reason, we seem to feel, for us to become angry with him. But emotion engenders emotion. When we react to anger with anger, our anger merely increases the anger of the other person. Our emotions tend to feed on one another until an impossible situation may develop.

The answer, according to both the biblical writer and social scientists, is simple. Don't react. Act. Learn to so discipline yourself that you can display a positive emotion in the face of a negative one. This means not only "turning the other cheek" but smiling when someone speaks curtly to you. But your "soft answer" is much more likely to "turn away wrath" than would an angry response.

Learn to Live with Criticism

When the late Frank W. Frueauff was president of a large utilities company, one of his junior executives committed the company to a large expenditure of money. Soon after the contract was signed, conditions changed drastically and the expenditure became almost a total loss to the company.

Other officials were highly critical of the man responsible for the loss. Although the responsible officer admitted his error, he felt keenly that the criticism he received was far stronger than he deserved.

Finally, in desperation, he went to Mr. Frueauff and asked if he did not feel that he was being criticized unjustly. "I don't know," Mr. Frueauff replied, "That isn't a question for me to answer. So far as I'm concerned it's water over the dam, and I've forgotten about it. But since the boys seem to be getting your goat, sit down and we'll talk about it a minute.

"I'll tell you what I'd do if I were in your place," he continued. "I'd consider this criticism for just what it's worth to me, regardless of whether it's good natured or otherwise. I'd make up my mind just what there is in it that is justifiable, if anything. If there's nothing in it, ignore it. Forget it altogether." [2]

From these wise words of Mr. Frueauff most of us can learn a valuable lesson. Throughout the course of life, all of us, at one time or another, will be subjected to severe criticism from things we have or have not done. The more positive we are in our actions, the more likely we are to be subjected to criticism. We can spend valuable time and emotional energy worrying unnecessarily over the criticism. But if we really want to do so, we can make even criticism a valuable learning opportunity.

Learning to live with criticism is one mark of emotional maturity. But we need a strategy for assessing and dealing with criticism. Simply "grinning and bearing it" is not enough. M. K. Wisehart [3] has proposed some questions for us to raise when we are under fire. The raising, answering, and acting upon these questions can help us learn some lessons from life which we can never learn in a schoolroom. The questions Mr. Wisehart proposes are the following:

1. What is the criticism?
2. Is it justifiable?
3. If not, is it the kind of criticism that is best ignored?
4. Assuming that the criticism is unjustified and should not be ignored, are there facts, unknown to my critics, that should be explained to them?
5. Assuming that the criticism is partly just, what does it tell me about my shortcomings or weaknesses?
6. Assuming that it is largely unjust, shall I not refrain from answering my critics until I have overcome the weakness or shortcoming which particularly justify their criticism?
7. Assuming that the criticism is entirely just and pertains to matters that are important to my success and to good relations with my friends and associates and others who are disposed to criticise me, what weaknesses must I overcome or what skills and experiences must I acquire to avoid similar criticism in the future?

Transform Tensions into Power

Ours has been described as a "step-lively-don't-block-traffic" civilization. We live in a "get results" culture in which the individual seemingly must move with the tide or get run over. The man who has time on his hands may be thought of as being unaggressive or something of an oddball. Someone has said that in order to be in tune with our times we have to be going somewhere—anywhere—under a full head of steam.

Consequently, the average person today is a bundle of tensions. As it sometimes is expressed, he is "tied up in knots on the inside." Many people never learn to live with their tensions. Their nerves become frayed, sleep becomes fitful, and physical or mental illness results. A person can take only a certain amount of tension. Just as metal has a "fatigue limit," each person has a limit to the amount of tension he can endure without disastrous consequences.

Fortunate is the person who has learned to transform tension into power. That "full head of steam" can be used either to destroy personality or to drive one on to great accomplishments. Many "under-dog" basketball teams have come out victorious in the big game simply because the players used their tensions as a motivating drive rather than a disrupting force. Most public speakers know that a certain amount of apprehension is needed to keep them at their best. Almost any successful businessman can attest to the fact that his fear of failure has been one of the most powerful forces which has driven him to success.

What lessons can we learn from dealing with tension? First, we can learn the value of planning our work. The next time you become nervous and wrought up over all the work you have to do, take time to plan your work carefully and observe the results. Energies which would otherwise be expended in nervous exasperation become channeled into creative activities which help get the job done. One successful professional man spends the last thirty minutes of each day planning and organizing his work for the next day. Throughout the evening, he is able to relax and enjoy other activities, for he has the assurance that his plans have been carefully made for the next day. Through planning ahead, to use an expression popularized by a management group, one is able to "work smarter not harder."

If we would convert tension into power, we need to learn to play. Wholesome physical recreation drains off nervous frustration and restores physical vigor. No one form of recreation is ideally suited to every person. Different types appeal to different people. The main thing is to find and to follow a regular schedule of wholesome recreation.

Adequate rest also helps transform tension into power. Persons close to the late John F. Kennedy attribute his indefatigable energy to his ability to relax, and even to catch a few winks of sleep, whenever there was time in his crowded schedule. No one ever outgrows his need for a sufficient amount of sleep at night. The relaxation and restoration which comes only through sleep is essential to the marshalling and right use of one's energies.

One of the most valuable lessons one can learn in dealing with tensions is that perspective and power come through meditation. When tension becomes a serious problem to us, usually we have not taken time to get a correct perspective of the situation we are facing. In the hurried, harried, work-a-day world, we need to take time to reflect on our daily activities in terms of long-range plans for life. The perspective we gain through such meditation not only helps to relieve tension but also gives a feeling of purposefulness essential to creative living.

Antidotes for Discouragement

Discouragement is a normal human experience. It comes to all of us from time to time. Although in an extreme form it may be a symptom of mental illness, for most of us it is something we endure occasionally.

But the fact that a certain amount of discouragement is inevitable does not mean that we should accept it as a fate about which we can do nothing. If we would live a happy, useful life, we need to develop skill in diagnosing the causes of discouragement and learn how to cope with it when it comes.

First of all, we need to realize that discouragement is a psychological condition. It is a state of mind. It may or may not flow from the experience of outward frustration. Even when it does have some basis in outward circumstances, frequently our inner emotions greatly exaggerate the external condition which stimulated them.

Moreover, Walker cautions:

. . . it is helpful to recognize that the human body runs in cycles. There are times when we are at the crest of physical efficiency and other times when the graph line hits bottom. Our physical low ties are reflected in our minds and spirits. . . .

It makes very little difference whether you are writing a book, singing, selling hardware, or playing baseball, there are times when you can't get a ball out of the infield. All you can manage is a little pop fly or a complete strike-out. It is discouraging and you would give almost anything to pull out of your slump. Then, without knowing why, you begin to tick again. You write with ease or you sing with power or you sell with relish and success. Quite possibly you have simply outrun a physical low and snapped back into good form.[4]

There are times, however, when discouragement does result directly from specific outward circumstances. We can identify those circumstances positively and describe them vividly. To cope with discouragement like this, we need to develop a philosophy of life which will help us through the rough spots. Often it helps to clarify our real purpose in life and to evaluate the unwanted circumstance in the light of our long-range objective. It may be helpful, too, to ask ourselves if the real problem is hurt pride. Many times a little honest reflection will force us to admit that the action which sent us spinning into a spell of discouragement was completely unintentional on the part of the person who committed it. In the event of prolonged discouragement, it is well to consider the possibility that physical or emotional fatigue is distorting our thinking and feelings.

There is no simple formula for overcoming all kinds of discouragement. The cause of the discouragement dictates the wise course to take to overcome it. If it is a mild discouragement which comes for no obvious reason, probably it will run its course in a short while. Vigorous physical exercise or some other pleasant diversion can help restore a wholesome outlook on life.

For prolonged or more intense discouragement, more drastic action may be needed. An outstanding accomplishment in another area may relieve frustration and restore law and order in one's psychic. The satisfaction of creating something, be it ever so humble, also can help. Even reviewing mentally one's personal achievements and assets can cause one to think less about liabilities and disadvantages. Claiming the promises of Christ gives strength to overcome when all else fails.

Finally, during hours of discouragement, remember that "the dark night of the soul" can be preparation for renewal. Out of deep anguish of the soul, with God's help, can come a capacity to live life on a higher, more useful level.

PERSONAL LEARNING ACTIVITIES

1. What valuable lessons have you learned from problems and crises you have experienced? Can you think of times when you experienced trials and failed to learn valuable lessons because of your negative attitude toward the circumstances?

2. During the next several days, observe your charac-

teristic reaction to criticism, curt remarks, or outright hostility expressed toward you. Make a deliberate effort to act positively rather than to react in the spirit which is expressed toward you.

3. Think through your philosophy of life and its adequacy in helping you deal with the trials and crises you will face in the future. If you find that your philosophy is inadequate, search for a meaningful philosophy which can help you meet the testing periods of life.

GROUP DISCUSSION STARTERS

1. Why do most adults find it so difficult to accept criticism? How can a person learn to become more objective in evaluating criticism by other persons?

2. What are some lessons we can learn from suffering which might not be learned in any other way?

3. What are some good ways to deal with discouragement?

4. What is meant by a "philosophy of life?" Does everyone have a philosophy of life? What kinds of beliefs should be included in one's philosophy of life?

NOTES

1. T. B. Mason, *Suffering: a Personal Perspective* (Nashville: Broadman Press, 1967), p. 4.

2. M. K. Wisehart, *Reading the Price Tags of Life* (New York: Halcyon House, 1938), p. 84.

3. *Ibid*, pp. 86–87.

4. Harold Blake Walker, *Power to Manage Yourself* (New York: Harper and Brothers Publishers, 1955), pp. 168–169.

CHAPTER 10
Is the Best Yet to Be?

In the opening chapter we saw how different our world today is from the world of a Virginia plantation owner fifty years ago. Whereas Big John Champion, the plantation owner, mastered his world by the time he was twenty years of age and, thereafter, had little need to continue to learn, our world today is changing too rapidly to be mastered by anyone. No longer is adulthood a time to quit learning and enjoy living. The adult today must continue to learn if he is to keep up with the world around him and avoid perpetual frustration, hopeless failure, and oblivion.

In this final chapter we will assess the need for adults to continue to learn during the years immediately ahead. Will the rate of change be slowed down so that adults soon can afford to relax their efforts to learn? Or, during the years immediately ahead, must the intelligent, well-adjusted adult accelerate his learning?

The answer to these questions depends, in part at least, upon the condition of our world during the 1970's and the 1980's. No one of us knows for sure what life will be like during the next two decades. On the one hand, we see ominous threats to our very existence in the form of racial conflicts, moral revolutions, and the threat of nuclear war. On the other hand, we hear reports, some glowing and some awesome, of changes we can expect as a result of radical developments in science and technology.

We see that our world is changing more rapidly and more dramatically each passing year. A regular plan for continuing to learn is not an option with today's adult. It is essential to survival.

The Secret of Successful Living

How can today's adult, through a continuing program of learning, make a satisfactory adjustment to a society changing at such a fantastic rate of speed. This is one of the most crucial questions facing twentieth-century man.

Of one thing we can be certain. It will be impossible for any one person to keep up with the knowledge explosion. It is estimated that man's total store of knowledge is doubling approximately every five years. Even though computers will help by storing and retrieving information as it is needed, few if any adults will be able to keep abreast of developments in all areas affecting their daily lives.

The only hope is for the adult to synergize his learning around crucial goals. Synergy is a medical term which means to combine or correlate action of different organs or parts of the body, as in performing complex movements. The well-adjusted adult of the future must organize daily learning activities around worthy life purposes in such a way that the informal learning experiences provide thrusts toward paramount goals in life.

Three goals are especially important to adults as they face tomorrow. They are (1) learning to adjust to change, (2) learning to stand for right on crucial issues, and (3) learning to live with the assurance of the unchanging realities of life.

1. Learning to Adjust to Change

First of all, we need to use our learning opportunities to help us adjust to change. Even though we may accept the fact that change is inevitable, many of us find the process of change painful. We are familiar with the traditional, and change threatens to thrust us into an uncertain world of the unknown.

Several kinds of creative learning experiences can help us to face such dilemmas. One of the most important of these is to get the facts. Through reading, talking with other persons, listening to the radio or TV, and other methods, we can find out as much as possible about all that is involved in the impending change. Many times our apprehensiveness and uncertainties are a result of a lack of knowledge. When we get all of the facts, the impending changes frequently don't seem nearly as ominous.

A second type of learning which can help us adjust to change is attitudinal. Yes, attitudes can be learned, and we need constantly to work at the task of developing an attitude of open-mindedness to impending change. Certainly not all change is good, but an attitude of open-mindedness even toward harmful change can help us appraise the proposed change and reach a defensible personal position. We need to realize that although unmanaged change becomes chaos, unchanged stability becomes stagnation.

Finally, we need to be willing to try experimental behavior to learn to adjust to change. In Germany it once was "proved" by experts that if a train traveled at the frightful speed of 15 miles per hour, blood would spurt from travelers' noses and passengers would suffocate going through tunnels. But a few brave souls were willing to attempt experimental behavior in riding at such a "terrific" rate of speed, and that which promised to be their doom revolutionized travel.

When change threatens us, a willingness to try experimental behavior often is the clue to progress.

2. Learning to Stand for Right

A prominent Southern newspaperman, in commenting on today's racial crisis, made a serious indictment of Christians. During this the greatest social revolution of our time, he asserted, church people, for the most part, have sat on the sidelines and watched changes taking place.

The day is rapidly approaching when intelligent adults, especially Christians, will be unable to sit on the sidelines and watch the world pass by. Issues in the area of Christian morality already have become so clear-cut that adults are finding it increasingly difficult not to take a stand either pro or con. During the years ahead, this trend will continue with new moral issues developing. The possibility of instant plebiscites on matters of civic interest will force adults into further stands.

Thus a worthy goal in life is to develop both the perception and the courage to take stands for the right on all issues of public concern. This calls for a continuing learning of facts on which to base judgments and a constant effort to develop skills in taking a stand.

3. Learning to Live with the Assurance of Unchanging Realities

In our day of uncertainty and change, the Christian adult needs to learn to live daily with deep confidence in the unchanging realities of life.

The greatest of these is the reality of God himself. Infinitely more powerful than all the force man can unleash in a thousand nuclear explosions is the power of the great Creator of the atom. This Creator established all natural law, and all that is going on in the world today involves man's use of principles and materials which God created.

We have the complete assurance, too, that God, the great Creator and Sustainer of the universe, loves each of us. The Bible says, "He careth for you" (1 Peter 5:7).

Man never achieves greater heights than when he is bowed in contrite prayer to God the great Creator. The Bible promises over and over that God will hear and answer the prayers of persons who love and seek to follow him.

These and many other unchanging truths which God has revealed to us can give strength and purpose to life during changing times. With the apostle Paul we, with complete confidence, can say: "I am certain that nothing can separate us from his love: neither death nor life; neither angels nor other heavenly rulers or powers; neither the present nor the future; neither the world above nor the world below—there is nothing in all creation that will ever be able to separate us from the love of God which is ours through Christ Jesus our Lord" (Rom. 8:38–39, TEV).

PERSONAL LEARNING ACTIVITIES

1. Analyze your characteristic reaction to change? How can you learn to adjust more satisfactorily to change?

2. How do you normally react to situations which call for you to take a stand which is unpopular? How can you learn to be more courageous in taking stands?

3. Think through and put in writing three unchanging truths which can give you assurance during crises.

GROUP DISCUSSION STARTERS

1. Why is it so difficult for the average adult to adjust to change? How can one discern good changes from bad changes? How can one learn to adjust to change?

2. What are some kinds of stands which Christian adults are called on to take? What are some general principles which one should try to follow in taking an unpopular stand?

3. What are some Scripture passages which give us the assurance that spiritual resources are available to help us face uncertainty and danger?

NOTES

1. *The Real Security,* a training film produced by the Bureau of National Affairs, 1341 24th Street, Washington, D. C.

2. *Executives Digest,* November, 1965 (Cambridge Associates, Inc.).